THE WAY

OF ECSTASY

THE *Way* OF ECSTASY

Praying with

PRAYING WITH
TERESA OF AVILA

Peter Tyler

MOREHOUSE PUBLISHING

Bible quotations are taken from The Jerusalem Bible.

Originally published in English under the title *The Way of Ecstasy*
by the Canterbury Press Norwich, St. Mary's Works, St. Mary's
Plain, Norwich, Norfolk NR3 3BH UK

Morehouse Publishing
P.O. Box 1321
Harrisburg, PA 17105

Morehouse Publishing is a division of The Morehouse Group.

Printed in the United States of America

Cover design by Corey Kent

Library of Congress Cataloging-in-Publication Data

Tyler, Peter, 1963–
    The way of ecstasy : praying with Teresa of Avila / Peter Tyler.
        p.   cm.
    Includes bibliographical references.
    ISBN 0-8192-1776-X (pbk.)
    1. Prayer—Christianity. 2. Teresa, of Avila, Saint, 1515–1582.
Moradas. I. Teresa, of Avila, Saint, 1515–1582. Moradas. English.
Selections. II. Title.
BV215.T85 1999
248.3—dc21   98-49910
                                                                CIP

To my mother and father

Contents

Acknowledgements

First and foremost, my thanks are due to Bishop Graham Chadwick and Christine Smith of the Canterbury Press for their support and encouragement in the preparation and writing of this book. Without their help it would not have been possible.

Endless conversations, workshops and discussions have contributed to the ideas expressed here and I am indebted to all who have shared their joy of inspiration in spirituality with me. In particular Hymie Wyse, Sima Sharma, Julienne McLean and Gerry Hughes. Many thanks to the latter for so kindly agreeing to write a foreword.

Many thanks to the clergy and parishioners of St Botolph's, Aldgate, and the staff and clients of St Botolph's Project for their constant support and encouragement. Also to the monks and parishioners of Christ the King, Cockfosters, and the Benedictine Centre for Spirituality, especially Dom Placid Meylink OSB.

Finally, thank you to all my friends and family for their unflagging enthusiasm at all times and who have contributed to the book in so many ways. Especially Gwynneth and Dido who kept the builders at bay.

Foreword

If you have ever asked yourself 'Who am I?' or 'What do I want out of life?' then this book will interest you. If you try even some of the many exercises which conclude each chapter, your interest will become engagement in ecstasy.

Ecstasy is a Greek word which literally means 'standing outside of'. Each of us sees the world from our own particular standpoint, which determines how we act and react to ourselves and to the world around us. Ecstasy means being moved away from our blinkered way of seeing to a new standpoint, from which we see ourselves and reality around us wonderfully differently. It is a seeing which transforms us.

True, transforming ecstasy cannot be achieved by drugs. The way to ecstasy is very ordinary, very arduous. St Teresa of Avila describes it through the metaphor of an interior castle, which contains seven mansions, corresponding to our stages of development in our journey to God. In this book, Peter Tyler offers a most enlightening commentary on St Teresa's work, *The Interior Castle*, bringing out her simplicity, homeliness, humour and earthiness which has so much practical wisdom to teach us today.

One very attractive feature of this book is the author's breadth of outlook. He makes connections between Teresa's teaching and the mystical teaching of other world religions, and also with the discoveries of depth psychology. At the end of the book he provides an extensive bibliography.

Peter Tyler is currently working with the homeless in London. He also spent years in L'Arche communities, has worked with drug addicts, alcoholics and AIDS victims. Such work is often called 'working on the margins of society'. From another standpoint – God's – it can be called 'working at the heart of the Kingdom'. It is because the author lives and writes out of this standpoint that his book is so powerful.

Gerard W. Hughes SJ
June 1997

Preface

This, then, is what I pray, kneeling before the Father, from whom every family, whether spiritual or natural, takes its name:

Out of his infinite glory, may he give you the power through his Spirit for your hidden self to grow strong, so that Christ may live in your hearts through faith, and then, planted in love and built on love, you will with all the saints have the strength to grasp the breadth and the length, the height and the depth; until, knowing the love of Christ, which is beyond all knowledge, you are filled with the utter fullness of God.

Glory be to him whose power, working in us, can do infinitely more than we can ask or imagine; glory be to him from generation to generation in the Church and in Christ Jesus for ever and ever. Amen.   Ephesians 3:14–21

Ecstasy: From the Greek *ek* and *stasis*: literally, 'to put out of place': *the state of being beside oneself, thrown into a frenzy or a stupor, with anxiety, astonishment, fear or passion* (OED).

The way of Teresa is the way of being put out of place, of seeing familiar things in an unfamiliar light, of being transfigured, transported; to delight in the ordinary and to rejoice in the simple wonder of the world we live in.

The intention of this book is to explore this way by using her little book, *The Interior Castle*, as a guide. It is not intended to be a substitute for reading Teresa in the original: she possesses a unique and lively style and will quickly draw you into her concerns and joys. If this book prompts you to read more of Teresa in the original then it will have achieved its purpose.

As part of the *Rhythm of Life* series it will explore Teresa's relevance to our world today.

I live in the heart of a big modern city, London, and find making time for prayer amongst the pressures of late twentieth-century life difficult and challenging at the best of times. Teresa has helped me find time for prayer and has guided my prayer life through her gentle advice. If you live in similar circumstances or if you enjoy more freedom and flexibility in your lifestyle I hope you will still find something of interest here. Although this book is not primarily intended for 'professional contemplatives' or Teresian scholars, I would be pleased to think that this introduction builds on their wonderful work and contributes something to making it known to a wider audience. To this end I include suggestions for further reading on pages 139–141.

Whilst writing I have become increasingly aware of the variety of interpretations to which Teresa's work is open. As you form your own impression of this extraordinary saint, I hope you will find pointers and signposts here to direct you in whichever way God is leading you. As Teresa might have said: *'Be guided as the waters!'*

Peter Tyler
London
Feast of the Holy Trinity, 1997

Introduction

Why Teresa?

In the evening you say, 'It will be fine; there is a red sky', and in the morning, 'Stormy weather today; the sky is red and overcast'. You know how to read the face of the sky, but you cannot read the signs of the times. Matthew 16:1–3

Teresa of Avila (or to give her her full name, *Teresa de Cepeda y Ahumada*) was a Spanish nun of the sixteenth century (she lived from 1515 to 1582). She spent all of her life in Spain, most of it in enclosed convents at a time when to be a nun meant a life of almost total seclusion from 'the world'. Those parts of her life that were not spent in convents were spent in the relative comfort of a reasonably wealthy family.

Spain during Teresa's lifetime was undergoing massive transformation. Only recently had 'the Moors' (Islamic Africans) been finally driven out from southern Spain and the Spanish were busy consolidating their ethnic and national identity, especially as defined in terms of the Christian religion in relation to the now minority Jewish and Islamic religions. In this context the now infamous Spanish Inquisition was working to promote consistency and purity amongst the Catholic faithful.

While all this was going on at home, abroad there was tumult and change. In Europe the Reformation had already begun and there was a constant battle for control between the new reforming movements

3

and the hegemony of the old Catholic settlement. Further afield, the New World had recently been discovered, and as the Conquistadors pushed forward the Spanish Empire deeper into the Americas, the gold and precious metals plundered from the native communities began to pour back into the Spanish coffers. Consequently, the wealth and power of Spain increased enormously during Teresa's lifetime. It was, metaphorically and literally, a 'golden age'; an age of change and excitement, the opening up of new worlds, while the old world, in the shape of medieval beliefs and outlook – especially in the Church – still survived with remarkable tenacity.

In many respects, then, it was a world totally unlike our own, and yet perhaps not so far removed from our own troubled times with its change and uncertainty: new things happening everywhere and a general sense of alarm as new technologies demand that people change their lifestyles. In Teresa's day, all this occurred against the backdrop of an ancient world, full of superstition and irrational belief. As in our own times, there was a general questioning of authority and the right of one group to claim control over another. In the Church in particular, there was widespread questioning of structures, who should hold power and why.

In recent years we have seen similar battles in our churches as to the nature of ministry and authority, especially in relation to groups traditionally excluded from power in the Church: women, underclasses both in the developed and developing worlds, and homosexuals, to name but three. We have become increasingly aware of the diversity of faith and can no longer ignore the fact that our faith does not exist in isolation. As in Teresa's day we are more aware than ever of the presence of other faiths and the need for dialogue and mutual understanding.

I have found that Teresa speaks to us as clearly now as she did to her contemporaries in sixteenth-century Spain. In a troubled world, where an old order is dying and a new one arising, she offers a way of discerning 'the signs of the times' and helps us to listen to the still, small voice of God amongst the thunder and cataclysms of the false voices that surround us.

Hers is a gentle way, a largely interior way, but one which leads back to 'the world'. It is a demanding way but one we can follow knowing that at its end is fulfilment in union with Christ. We may have to question many of our assumptions and as we are led 'out of ourselves' we shall discover that true ecstasy lies in the rediscovery of the obvious, that which lay before us all along. Before we explore her way, which she described in *The Interior Castle*, we shall recall the main events of her life.

Chapter 1

Fire from Heaven

I have come to bring fire to the earth, and how I wish it were blazing already!   Luke 12:49

Family Secrets

Some years ago I was lucky enough to spend a holiday in central Spain and had the chance to visit Teresa's home, Avila. As the old song has it: 'The rain in Spain falls mainly on the plain'; and if you have ever travelled through central Spain you will know just how much plain there is. We set off on a gloriously hot August morning and travelled for mile after mile in magnificent open plain more akin to Africa than Europe. On either side were spectacular fields of sunflowers and we half expected Don Quixote and Sancho Panza to appear at any moment to tilt at a windmill!

Eventually the city of Avila, 'Avila of the Knights', loomed up before us. Glittering and shimmering in the early morning sun, it truly appeared like something from *The Interior Castle*. Avila was Teresa's home for most of her life, and if she was not actually living there it remained a base or anchor-point. During the Middle Ages it had been a Christian stronghold in the battles with the Moors and had a reputation as a place of chivalry and courage.

Although Teresa's family was impeccably Christian and quite well-to-do, the apparent respectability concealed a dark family secret:

6

Teresa's grandfather, Juan Sanchez, had been Jewish. Not only Jewish but a Jew who joined the *conversos*: those who had converted to Christianity and were usually referred to uncharitably by their established Christian brethren as *marranos* – literally, 'pigs'.

It was to check the activities of such converts that the Spanish Inquisition had been established and in 1485 they were busy in Toledo, home of Teresa's grandfather. He was found guilty of offences concerning reversion to the Jewish faith (probably something simple like refusing to eat pork) and was paraded through the streets of Toledo in humiliation.

Living in the century of Hitler and the Jewish Holocaust all this will sound horribly familiar. Film footage of the humiliation of intellectuals, writers and dissidents by the Red Guard in China in the 1960s also bears a chilling similarity to the woodcuts we have of the humiliations of Jews and heretics at the hands of the authorities before the terrifying *autos de fé*: public burning, usually in the town square. Juan Sanchez was lucky enough to be spared execution and soon after fled to Avila to rebuild his life with a new name and ancestry purchased at considerable price.

Juan's son, Alonso, married well: first to a lady of impeccable Christian pedigree, Catalina del Peso y Heñao, and later, after she had died, to the fourteen-year-old Beatriz de Ahumada, who was to bear him nine children before dying exhausted in 1528. Juan and Alonso did such a good cover-up job on their ancestry that the Jewish link was not discovered until 1947. Indeed in 1597, fifteen years after Teresa's death, the reformed congregation she had formed, the Discalced Carmelites, passed a decree forbidding anyone joining who had Jewish or Moorish ancestry back to the fourth generation.[1]

Some commentators have detected in Teresa's writing and spirituality more than a hint of the symbolism and learning of the Jewish Kabbala and mystical writings of the late Middle Ages. Did she do this intentionally, or had she perhaps overheard secret things in her childhood? Or were they her dual spiritual inheritance re-emerging through her writing? We shall probably never know.

The Wild Child and the Nun

'Sensual', 'exuberant', 'ecstatic' and 'carefree' are just a few of the adjectives that are used to describe Teresa. Of all the saints and holy men and women throughout the history of the Church she stands out as someone warm and loving. As a child she loved to play and run and as a teenager she embraced with delight all the attractions and diversions available to cultured young ladies of her time. She sang, danced and played the tambourine and lute exquisitely; she rode, played chess and joined in all the local gossip and fun. In her famous autobiographical *Life*, she tells us:

> I began to deck myself out and to try to attract others by my appearance, taking great trouble with my hands and hair, using perfumes and all the vanities I could get – and there were a good many of them, for I was very fastidious.[2]

Writing about these events later as a fifty year old, she chastises herself and condemns her vain behaviour. Yet she never lost her vitality, even into

8

old age. Throughout her writings the vivacious, heady teenager is never far below the surface.

Apart from marriage, there were very few career options for women in Spain in the sixteenth century. Teresa took one of the best on offer: joining a convent. Deeply spiritual and drawn to a life of prayer and contemplation, after a period at an Augustinian convent she entered the Convent of the Incarnation in Avila in November 1536.

It is difficult to imagine what life would have been like in such a convent; the quality of life for each sister depended very much on the circumstances of the family she had come from (even the religious houses of the time were not immune to the social distinctions and categories that dominated Spain in the sixteenth century). Thus, whereas Teresa was given a suite of rooms with bedroom, kitchen, oratory and guestroom, the daughters of poorer families slept in a common dormitory and essentially acted as skivvies to their more distinguished sisters. At the time Teresa thought nothing of this inequality, but in later years she would come to realize its pitfalls.

Considering Teresa's background and ancestry there are two ironic things about the convent she had chosen to join. First, the large, rambling house on the outskirts of Avila (there were 130 women at the time that Teresa joined) was located on the ruins of the old Jewish cemetery. Secondly, the order she had chosen – the Carmelites – had its roots in the Jewish Old Testament. The feats accomplished on Mount Carmel by the prophets Elijah and Elisha had made the mountain a holy place, attractive to hermits – many of whom were retired crusader knights.

Between 1206 and 1214 the hermits were given a rule by the Latin Patriarch of Jerusalem, Albert. His *Primitive Rule of the Order of the Blessed Virgin Mary of Mount Carmel* is a model of simplicity and refinement to which Teresa was drawn throughout her life.

For twenty years, then, Teresa lived as a daughter of Carmel in her chosen convent. Life was certainly far from austere, although it was not the comfortable life she would have found at home. Townsfolk frequently came to the convent to gossip and chat and the nuns would often go away for long periods on their own. Teresa revelled in it all and proved immensely popular and sociable. However, a shadow soon fell across her young life. Just after her profession of vows in 1538 her health collapsed and she fell into a catatonic state. In August 1539, after a series of well-meant but misguided 'cures', her Requiem Mass was celebrated at another convent of the order! Reports of her death, however, proved to be exaggerated and after a few months she was on the road to recovery. It was three years before she was fully restored, and during this time her priorities began to change. She found she was more drawn to prayer than to the pleasurable diversions she had previously enjoyed.

Visions of Ecstasy

We know very little about Teresa's life in the convent over the next fifteen years or so and have to rely on her *Life* to provide the missing details. What is clear is that through a process of self-discipline and divine inspiration Teresa began to enjoy spiritual favours the like of which she had never known. By the 1550s she regularly experienced the locutions, visions, levitations and ecstasies for which she is famous. The most well-known of these is 'The Transverberation of the Heart' (it was the basis for Bernini's famous erotic statue in Rome). Teresa described the experience in her *Life*:

It pleased the Lord that I should sometimes see the following vision. I would see beside me, on my left hand, an angel in bodily form – a type of vision which I am not in the habit of seeing, except very rarely. Though I often see representations of angels, my visions of them are of the type which I first mentioned. It pleased the Lord that I should see this angel in the following way. He was not tall, but short, and very beautiful, his face so aflame that he appeared to be one of the highest types of angel who seem to be all afire.... In his hand I saw a long golden spear and at the end of the iron tip I seemed to see a point of fire. With this he seemed to pierce my heart several times so that it penetrated to my entrails. When he drew it out, I thought he was drawing them out with it and he left me completely afire with a great love for God. The pain was so sharp that it made me utter several moans; and so excessive was the sweetness caused me by this intense pain that one can never wish to lose it, nor will one's soul be content with anything less than God. It is not bodily pain, but spiritual, though the body has a share in it. So sweet are the colloquies of love which pass between the soul and God that if anyone thinks I am lying I beseech God, in His goodness, to give him the same experience.[3]

11

In modern psychological terms we would call this a 'peak experience' and as we read the above account something of the fire, passion and ecstasy of Teresa's personality comes to life.

A cynical commentator today may write off Teresa's experience as the ravings of a sexually frustrated woman, yet that would be to miss entirely the point of the role of *eros* in her life. This Greek word from which we derive our word *erotic* is often today associated purely with physical, sexual love. However, in its original Greek sense it meant 'the power that brings things together'.

In our own century, the psychoanalyst Freud postulated that there were two forces operating in our lives: the death instinct that seeks the dissolution and destruction of all things, and *eros* (or libido) – the energy that wells up from a deep, hidden source within us and brings things together, enabling us to connect with the cosmos around us. The American Carmelite, William McNamara, has put it thus:

> Eros pertains essentially to the art of making love (*coming into union – communion*). Sex is limited to the manipulation of organs. Eros attracts and lures us into union with everything. Eros is wakeful, vigilant, remembering whatever is true and beautiful, whatever is good. Sex is a need; eros is desire. The sex act is, indeed, the most potent symbolic and specific celebration of relatedness imaginable. But eros is relatedness. Excitement accompanies sex. Tenderness dominates the erotic quest.
>
> Eros is the longing to enjoy such deep and wide-ranged dimensions of relatedness – all

originating from a critical centre and tending toward an ultimate end – that ... [an] erotic desire for union plays a central part in man's rapport with animal and plant life, as well as with aesthetic, philosophical, ethical, scientific, socio-political and religious forms. Eros relates us not only to other persons whom we love, but to the pig we are raising, the house we are building, the car we are driving, the vocation we are following.[4]

Eros, the passion that drives us and brings us into union with one another and with the earth around us, was the passion that drove Teresa and flowed out in her ecstasies. From this point on in her life she was in communion with that energy and used it to change forever the nature of the religious life she had embarked upon.

Change in the Air

By the late 1550s change was in the air. Teresa was now well settled into a strict and balanced regime of prayer and meditation. Because of the visions and ecstasies she experienced she became something of a local celebrity. People would come to the convent to see if they could catch a glimpse of Teresa in one of her ecstasies. There were many eye-witness accounts of her levitations given as testimonies to her sainthood after her death. We can make of them what we will today. Teresa's attitude was completely matter-of-fact about it all and she saw these 'incidentals' as only having meaning and value within the context of a simple life of prayer and good works.

Accompanying her visions, however, was a deep desire for a more austere and simple living space.

She set her heart on nothing less than her own convent based on the original primitive vision of the Carmelite rule. (The Carmelites of her day practised a 'mitigated rule' that dispensed them from some of the more rigorous aspects of the original rule.) Thus in 1558 Teresa, assisted by a small group of like-minded sisters, including two of her nieces, began preparations to instigate a new 'primitive' convent in Avila.

From now until the end of her life her name would be associated with this reform of the Carmelite order: the so-called 'discalced' reform (literally 'shoeless', from the fact that her sisters did not wear shoes in the convents).

Teresa and her allies knew the way forward would not be smooth; the people of Avila probably thought they already had enough convents and the thought of more mouths to feed would not be welcomed (sisters at the time did not earn their livings but relied on the giving of alms from those outside the order).

Eventually, early in the morning of 24 August 1562, a new sound was heard amongst the church bells of Avila: the little handbell of Teresa's new Convent of St Joseph's. Accompanied by various well-wishers, Teresa and the first four sisters of the reform said their morning prayers together.

Within hours there was uproar as news travelled around the town and within two days a meeting of the City Council (including representatives of the religious orders of Avila) was held at which it was decided that the convent must be shut down. Despite an attempt at a forced eviction that afternoon the Council was unsuccessful and had to resort to the law courts to get their way. The case dragged on for another two years and only in 1563 was Teresa finally allowed to settle in the new convent. The reform of the Carmelites had finally begun.

Why were the people of Avila so angry at Teresa? It is perhaps difficult to understand the strength of their reaction, living as we do in a time of apathy towards religious matters. Avila in Teresa's day would have been a small, tightly-knit community where everyone knew everyone else's business and where a change in the status quo would have been seen as criticism, implied or otherwise, of accepted norms. The nuns at Teresa's old convent of the Incarnation would probably have felt that Teresa considered them less spiritual or devoted than herself and her followers.

This pattern was to repeat itself for the remainder of her life: selecting a location, making preparations in secret, a sudden opening accompanied by public opposition, followed gradually and slowly by acceptance. A large degree of the success of her reform lay in Teresa's own personality: her combination of personal charm and an eye for practical details made all the difference, and she was able to persuade the most influential people to help her work. She was as at home in the rich Spanish court of her day as she was with the simple tradesmen and craftsmen with whom she dealt in the furnishing and establishment of her convents. Her later book, *The Book of Her Foundations*, chronicles the stories of these convents and the colourful events of her travels.

Despite these initial difficulties at Avila, Teresa called the next four-and-a-half years (1563–67) 'the most restful years of my life' and indeed they were.

She devoted herself with all her motherly skills to the establishment of her new little convent – as simple and practical as can be imagined.

Often non-Christians find the pomp, grandeur and riches of cathedrals and churches difficult to accept. 'What has this got to do with Christ?' they say. 'How can you call yourself a follower of Christ when he possessed nothing and had "nowhere to lay his head"?' This has been asked thoughout the history of Christianity and has been the inspiration of reforming movements such as Teresa's. If you go to her original house today you will see how literally she took Christ's poverty as an example. In this respect she has a lot to teach us today.

As well as prayer, administration and care of her sisters (including organizing lively recreations with singing and dancing), Teresa began her writing career in earnest with her first two completed works: *The Life* (her autobiography) and *The Way of Perfection*.

Even in translation her passion and spirit come across and she writes about the most sublime spiritual things with the simplest and most homely of metaphors. She often uses water to illustrate spiritual matters (we shall return to this later); at other times she gives the analogy of the spiritual life as being like a bullfight, or a game of chess – very racy metaphors for a nun of her time! Coupled with this is sound and practical advice together with a shrewd understanding of human nature and its weaknesses.

Religious communities, despite an outward appearance of calm and order to the outside world, can often be a seething hotbed of faction, conflict and deceit. Thus in her writings she frequently stresses the need to be on our guard for such spiritual pride and duplicity. In *The Way of Perfection* she has short shrift for such behaviour:

> If one of you should be cross with another because of some hasty work, the matter must at once be put right and you must betake yourselves to earnest prayer. The same applies to the harbouring of any grudge, or to party strife, or to the desire to be greatest, or to any nice point concerning your honour. (My blood seems to run cold as I write this, at the very idea that this can ever happen, but I know it is the chief trouble in convents.) If it should happen to you, consider yourselves lost. ...
>
> Oh, what a great evil is this! God deliver us from a convent into which it enters: I would rather our convent caught fire and we were all burned alive.[5]

She could be tough as well as loving and it was this special blend of compassion and steel that made her such a good foundress.

On the Road

From 1567 to the end of her life Teresa was constantly on the move, founding new houses, getting involved with ecclesiastical politics, or spending time organizing and instructing her growing band of sisters. It is from this period of her life that the famous anecdote occurs of how one day, after a long and hard journey in the covered wagon in which she travelled the length and breadth of Spain, she stepped out of the wagon only to fall head over heels into a pool of mud (if not something more unpleasant from the mules). Looking up to heaven she is reported to have said: 'Well God, if this is how you treat your friends, no wonder you've got so few of them!'

In 1567 she had founded a new house in Medina del Campo, swiftly followed in the next few years with foundations at Valladolid, Malagon, Toledo (where her grandfather had been humiliated all those years before), Salamanca, Segovia and elsewhere.

In the same year Teresa first encountered one of the most influential people in her life: the young mystic we now know as St John of the Cross. He was twenty-five when she met him in Medina (she was fifty-two), yet she immediately recognized his great spiritual gifts and proposed that he help her in establishing a male version of her reform, an invitation he accepted. They got on famously and Teresa jokingly referred to him as her 'half friar' on account of his diminutive stature. Yet John was a powerful, inspiring figure. He had a maturity beyond his years. He had been brought up in poor hardship and in his teenage years worked as nurse-porter in the Medina hospital that offered special assistance to people with syphilis – the new venereal disease which had arisen from contacts with the New World and was wreaking havoc amongst the young and sexually active at the time. (This would be the equivalent of working in an AIDS hospice today.) At an early age John would have encountered extremes of human suffering.

The titles of John's writings – *The Dark Night of the Soul*, *The Living Flame of Love*, *The Spiritual Canticle*, *The Ascent of Mount Carmel* – convey something of the passion of his style. He is sometimes referred to as the 'Prince of Mystics'.

July 1571 saw an extraordinary event: Teresa was elected prioress of her old alma mater, the Convent of the Incarnation. The convent was exactly divided as to those who supported her and those who opposed her, so that when she arrived on the 10 July to take up her position there were riots both inside and outside the convent. Elizabeth Ruth Obbard describes it in her biography *La Madre*:

> When Teresa's party arrived outside the church pandemonium issued from within the enclosure. The stoutest nuns tried to block the entrance, others shrieked and shook their fists defiantly, one fainted in the crush. A small faction who wanted their new prioress intoned the *Te Deum* above the noise. Teresa quietly passed through the hubbub and knelt before the altar in the choir.[6]

Once safely inside Teresa set about the slow and careful job of reconciliation, reconstruction and reform and her first act of reconciliation was a stroke of genius. When the nuns assembled later that afternoon for the inauguration of the prioress they found that she was not occupying the prioress's stall in chapter – rather, she had placed a life-size statue of the Virgin Mary in the stall, holding the convent keys. Teresa herself sat crouching on the floor, feet neatly tucked under her habit. She then addressed the sisters in these famous words:

> My ladies, mothers and sisters: Our Lord has sent me to this house, by virtue of obedience, to hold this office, which I had never thought of and which I am far from deserving.

19

This election has greatly distressed me, both
because it has laid upon me a task which I shall
be unable to perform, and also because it has
deprived you of the freedom of election which you
used to enjoy and given you a prioress whom you
would not have chosen at your will and pleasure,
and a prioress who would be accomplishing a
great deal if she could succeed in learning from
the least of you here all the good that is in her.[7]

Within months peace had been declared and
Teresa started to win over the hearts of her erst-
while sisters.

In 1572 she appointed John of the Cross as
confessor to the nuns (he had now acquired his own
reputation as a revered holy man). The welcome
appointment was inspired and did much to consoli-
date the work she was doing. Worse troubles lay
ahead, however, and both Teresa and John would be
tested to the limits in the years left to them.

Storms and Disaster: The Dark Night

1575 got off to a good start for Teresa. In February
she arrived with a party of sisters to begin a new
foundation in the Castilian town of Beas. Here she
was to meet another young man who was to play a
major role in her final ten years. Jerome Gratian
(known as 'Gratian') was a young friar, twenty-eight
years old. There was an immediate rapport and
over the coming years they were to support each
other in all the troubles that were to come. And
troubles there were.

While Teresa was undergoing her work of reform,
all manner of political events were fomenting. In

sixteenth-century Spain, politics, in-fighting and intrigue played a large role in the day-to-day life of religious orders.

The chief actors on the stage were the head of the Carmelite order in Spain, the head of the order in Rome, the Pope and the King of Spain, Philip II. Depending on who held greatest power at the time and their opinion of Teresa and her reform, her fortunes waxed and waned. In 1575 the alignment of factions was such that the reform lost favour, and at a General Chapter of the Order that year the unreformed ('Calced') friars won the day and decrees were issued which were designed to stop further reform.

Thus, Teresa was forbidden from founding any new convents and she was ordered to 'retire' indefinitely to a convent of her choice in Castille – effectively becoming a prisoner. Teresa obeyed and returned to the place of her ancestors – Toledo. There she sat out the troubles, continuing her battles from behind the convent walls by letters, persuasion and writing.

Her companion, John of the Cross, was spared this luxury. In scenes which seem shocking to us today, he was kidnapped by his fellow monks on 3 December 1577 and held prisoner in a cell of a Calced monastery in Toledo for nine months. His cell was 10ft by 6ft and had been used as a latrine. He lived on sardines, bread and water, and each evening, after the monks had finished supper, he was taken up to the refectory where the monks had an opportunity to flog him publicly. In these appalling conditions he wrote some of his greatest poems, and underwent an extraordinary deepening of his spiritual insight. John was taken to the very edge of sanity and decency and there met God in a new and all-consuming way. This experience would become the basis of his majestic writings exploring the darkness of unknowing. While John was producing his great works Teresa, also, turned to her inner resources. At this time of crisis when her whole life work seemed to be in ruins she managed to produce one of her greatest works: *The Interior Castle* (in Spanish *Las Moradas – The Mansions*). This extraordinary little book of mysticism, poetry, practical advice and perceptive psychology is truly her masterpiece – and she wrote it in just eight weeks. It is as relevant and readable today as it was then and we will be using it as our guide for the interior spiritual journey for the rest of this book.

'An Old Crone'

Finally, by courage, perseverance and the grace of God, the tide was turned and both Teresa and John were allowed to return to their normal lives. (John, however, executed a dramatic escape from his prison, using, so it is said, tied-up blankets and the aid of a little dog!)

As soon as she could Teresa was travelling again, founding new convents and giving encouragement to her established ones. She now called herself 'an old crone', recognizing her age and frailty – yet despite this she was in greater demand than ever and offers to found new convents came pouring in.

John, having escaped his tormentors, was able to write and minister again, but the privations he had experienced turned out to be too much – he died at the early age of forty-nine in 1591. Teresa herself struggled on, but it was clear that she was coming to the end of the road. In 1582, arriving home after a long and tiring journey, she was asked by the Duchess of Alba to attend the labour of her daughter-in-law so that the delivery would be blessed by the presence of the saint. After a tedious and difficult journey she arrived at the Duchess's castle only to be told that the child had been born and her presence was no longer required. Her response was characteristic: 'God be praised, there will be no need for this saint now!'

Desperate to get back to her beloved Avila she was unable to finish the journey due to her frailty and exhaustion and she was taken to the nearby convent of Alba where she declined rapidly. She died at nine o'clock on 4 October 1582, having exclaimed as she received the Blessed Sacrament the evening before:

O my Lord and Spouse! This is the longed-for hour, it is time now that we should see each other again, my Beloved and my Lord, it is time now that I should go to Thee; let us go in peace, and may thy holy will be done. Now the hour has come for me to leave this exile, and to enjoy thee whom I have so much desired.[8]

The hidden one was about to reveal himself.

After her death this verse was found on a book-mark amongst her belongings:

Let nothing disturb you,
Let nothing frighten you,
All things pass away:
God never changes.

23

Patience obtains all things.
The one who has God
Lacks nothing;
God alone suffices.

St Teresa's Bookmark

Exercise One

Rediscovering Eros

Set half an hour aside, find a quiet place and use some of the stillness exercises in the appendix to centre yourself.

When you are in a peaceful state allow the events of your life to roll past you like a film. Dwell on any events that are significant and let different characters speak to you at different times. This may take some time and you may need to spread it over several sessions. For some people writing things down may help (as they seemed to for Teresa). Resist the temptation to write while you are contemplating, but write things down when the session has finished.

Try and locate the 'passion' in your life – where is the energy that has driven you to union with other people, with nature, with art, or with God? What are the things that you strongly desire and how do you express your passion? Concentrate also on the areas where you block passion: the events, people, situations or ideas that you avoid or repress for fear of the consequences. You may like to write them down.

Imagine that you are talking to Christ about these passions and blocks. Talk to him about their joys and their dangers or pitfalls. If some desires make you unhappy, ask for his help in sorting them out.

You may want to bring Teresa into the discussion – I'm sure she'll have plenty of good suggestions. Perhaps some of the situations she encountered resemble your own. Consider how she coped with them and whether she has any advice for you.

When you are ready, finish the imaginary conversation and open your eyes. Notice how you feel now and be aware of your reactions to any suggestions that may have been made in these dialogues. If you are comfortable with the idea, you may want to talk about this exercise further with a close friend or spiritual 'soulmate' – we will talk more about this in a later chapter.

*

If you found the experience puzzling or you found it difficult to enter into, don't worry, just note that and move on. We will have plenty of opportunities to cover these areas later on.

Chapter 2

The First Mansion:
Entering the Castle

One Cold Night

On a cold wintry night in 1579 Teresa, whilst travelling with three of her nuns through a heavy snowstorm, sought refuge in an inn. To her great surprise and delight she discovered that one of her old friends, Fray Diego de Yepes was already installed there. (Being a priest he had, of course, been given the best rooms!) He immediately gave up his suite for the sisters and the little party made itself comfortable and settled in for the night. The next day they were completely snowed-in, so the day was spent in relaxation, prayer and conversation.

In this snowbound inn, Teresa divulged to Fray Diego the original vision that had inspired *The Interior Castle*. Many years later he recalled the moment in a letter to a friend:

This holy Mother had been desirous of obtaining some insight into the beauty of a soul in grace. Just at that time she was commanded to write a treatise on prayer, about which she knew a great deal from experience. On the eve of the festival of the Most Holy Trinity she was thinking what subject she should choose for this treatise, when

God, who disposes all things in due form and order, granted this desire of hers, and gave her a subject. He showed her a most beautiful crystal globe, made in the shape of a castle, and containing seven mansions, in the seventh and innermost of which was the King of Glory, in the greatest splendour, illumining and beautifying them all. The nearer one got to the centre, the stronger was the light; outside the palace limits everything was foul, dark and infested with toads, vipers and other venomous creatures.

While she was wondering at this beauty, which by God's grace can dwell in the human soul, the light suddenly vanished. Although the King of Glory did not leave the mansions, the crystal globe was plunged into darkness, became as black as coal and emitted an insufferable odour, and the venomous creatures outside the palace boundaries were permitted to enter the castle.

This was a vision which the holy Mother wished that everyone might see, for it seemed to her that no mortal seeing the beauty and splendour of grace, which sin destroys and changes into such hideousness and misery, could possibly have the temerity to offend God. It was about this vision that she told me on that day, and she spoke so freely both of this and of other things that she realized herself that she had done so and on the next morning remarked to me: 'How I forgot myself last night! I cannot think how it happened. These desires and this love of mine made me lose all sense of proportion. Please God they may have done me some good!' I promised her not to repeat what she had said to anyone during her lifetime.[1]

This beautiful account gives us the main themes of the journey we are about to embark upon. There is the castle itself – beautiful and shining, glittering mysteriously as it hovers over us, beckoning us to enter. There are the dark forces outside, especially the lizards and toads. These are kept at bay by God's grace but able to enter at a moment's notice. There is the drama, the sudden changes of light and dark, as though a summer storm has suddenly erupted. Then the smells and feelings and sensations: now of gladness, now of fear. There are the seven crystal spheres or mansions, each containing a message and a lesson. Finally there is Christ himself, waiting at the centre in great beauty and majesty, the goal of all our longings.

The colourful language may sound strange to our twentieth-century ears, but what Teresa is trying to do is to describe the most fundamental processes of the human soul – through image, picture and analogy. Throughout the journey of the castle there are many images and often she uses several at the same time.

Thus we encounter water, fire, the crystal spheres, butterflies, devils, lizards, transformation, the dark night and finally, at the end of all our seeking, the vision of the mystical marriage as our soul finds union with God himself.

It is a journey of surprises, full of dangers and delights and every bit as exciting as a Hollywood adventure film. Let us enter the castle, then, and begin our journey.

Knocking on the Door

Having conjured up the image of the castle, Teresa

28

now encourages us to enter it. What does she mean by this? She herself acknowledges:

> I seem to be talking such nonsense, for there can clearly be no question about entering it, since this castle is the soul. We ourselves are the castle! How silly to tell someone to enter a room he is in already![2]

Yet 'prayer and meditation are the gate into this castle', which is to say that we have here a guided fantasy or imaginative exercise through a world such as we find in dreams. At the end of this chapter you will find a guided exercise to emulate the sort of thing Teresa is trying to get across here.

For now, imagine yourself on a hot summer's day walking through a beautiful, lush meadow. Notice the flowers, the blue skies, the butterflies; the sounds and scents of summer. Feel the warm sun on your thin summer clothes.

Now imagine yourself walking out of the meadow into a dark cave or a cold, dark church. Notice how you can't see anything at first and how after a few moments the warmth of your clothes melts away and the cold damp begins to enter your bones. You feel disorientated and distressed, and probably regretful that you decided to come into such a gloomy place on such a gorgeous day. Perhaps you can still hear the sounds of people outside, playing tennis, or laughing and generally enjoying themselves.

This is Teresa's description of our first entry into the castle, which is her way of describing what it is like to begin praying after a long absence from prayer, or having had no experience of prayer whatsoever.

People often ask me 'How do you learn to pray?' or 'What is the best way of praying?' These are very difficult questions to answer as prayer is such a personal thing – there are as many ways of praying as there are people! It is interesting what Jesus says in St Luke's Gospel when asked the same question:

One day Jesus was praying in a certain place. When he finished, one of his disciples said to him, 'Lord, teach us to pray, just as John taught his disciples.' He said to them, 'When you pray, say: "Father,
hallowed be your name,
your kingdom come.
Give us each day our daily bread.
Forgive us our sins,
for we also forgive everyone who sins against us.
And lead us not into temptation" ...
So I say to you: Ask and it will be given to you; seek and you will find; knock and the door will be opened to you. For everyone who asks receives; he who seeks finds; and to him who knocks; the door will be opened.
Luke 11:1–4, 9–10 (New International Version)

We must knock – hammer if need be – on our inner door, the door of our inner castle, and demand entrance – assured that this will be granted, no matter how unworthy we may consider ourselves. And while we knock, we must say to ourselves: *What am I looking for? What do I really want out of life? What is my deepest desire?*

For Teresa's journey is a journey of desire and it is only in befriending our desires that we can find happiness.

30

The Lizards

What happens once we enter? Teresa describes it thus:

> The light from the King's chamber hardly shines at all in this First Mansion. Although the rooms are not as pitch dark as they were when the soul was in a state of sin, they are still very gloomy, so that very little can be seen. I don't know how to explain this properly. It's not that there's anything wrong with the rooms, but they're full of snakes, vipers and poisonous reptiles. These loathsome creatures have come in from outside the castle and it's because of them that the soul can't see the light. It's as though someone enters a room full of brilliant sunshine, and can hardly see a thing because her eyes are all clogged up with dirt. In the same way, those fierce, wild creatures have blocked the soul's vision, to everything but themselves.[3]

What are these 'lizards' and 'loathsome creatures' she describes here? A little further on she refers to the 'possessions, money, recognition, work' that prevent us from taking time to 'stand still and gaze at the beautiful castle' which *is* what we would really like to do.

These things are important and it would be foolish to try to live without them, but at the beginning of the spiritual journey they can be an unnecessary distraction which will stop us entering into a real encounter with God.

Teresa's near contemporary, St Ignatius of Loyola, says at the beginning of his *Spiritual Exercises* that

31

we should ideally preserve a state of 'indifference or non-attachment' to these created things, only being swayed to what will lead to a greater praise and reverence of God. It could be argued that the sign of a true spiritual person is not how much they renounce the world, but how much they stand in right relation to the world, appreciating its many gifts and wonders and thanking God for them:

> For this is the word of the Lord,
> The creator of heaven,
> The God who made earth and shaped it,
> He who made it firm.
> He did not make it in vain,
> He made it to be lived in.
> *'I am the Lord, there is no other,*
> *I have not spoken in secret, in some dark place.*
> *I have not said to Jacob's sons*
> *"Search for me in vain."'*   Isaiah 45:18–19

In a famous analogy, Teresa compares the position of one who prays to that of someone who sits and watches a bullfight: one who doesn't pray is in the position of the one actually in the ring being gored by the bull. The pray-er can sit and observe the terrible attacks of life but still preserve a sense of proportion and balance.

In the Hindu *Upanishads*, the ancient sacred texts of India, the human soul is compared to two birds that sit on a branch. One sits and eats the fruit on the branch, whereas the other sits further back and observes the first. This is to say that part of ourselves is committed and engaged in action in the world, but another part will always be separate and distinct and will preserve a certain serenity.

This is the part of ourselves that we cultivate during prayer and meditation. For the sages of old, a balanced and peaceable existence was to be found through cultivating a balance between these two parts.

This attitude of necessary balance runs throughout Teresa's work. Hers is a gentle way, and her Lord and Master is gentle. As St Benedict says in his *Rule*, it is important that we do not destroy the pot as we try to remove the rust.

I think the point Teresa is trying to get across in her image of the lizards invading the castle is that we become obsessed and upset the balance of the whole by being too concentrated on one small part.

How often have you gone to bed at night, worried about something, almost to the point of distraction, only to find when you wake the next morning that it wasn't important at all? This is the tendency Teresa is describing here, that we can become obsessed with new cars, boyfriends or girlfriends, or better jobs. These are the 'lizards' that invade us – invade the castle – as we struggle to find meaning in our lives.

Know Thyself!

Some of the experiences a beginner to prayer can expect to encounter are described by Teresa as very beautiful, such as the vision of the crystal sphere (and frequently a journey of prayer will begin in this way). Less pleasant experiences may follow, however, as the distractions and worries of our lives come tumbling in and 'invade the castle walls'.

Teresa counsels 'perseverance, humility and self-knowledge' in equal measure. In fact, if there is one overriding theme in her way it is the need for self-knowledge and how lack of it leads to misery and delusion:

> O Lord, remember how much we have to suffer on this road because of our own ignorance.... And so we go through dreadful trials because we don't understand our own nature, and worry over supposedly serious faults that in reality are not only harmless but good. This is the cause of so much suffering by many who practise prayer, and it is felt particularly by the unlearned. They complain of interior trials, become depressed, their health deteriorates and they may even give up prayer altogether, all because they fail to perceive the interior world that we have within ourselves.... Most of our anxieties and troubles come because we don't understand ourselves.[4]

In the light of this knowledge, bad experiences will slowly begin to make sense as the total picture emerges. For the time being we must heed the cry of the philosopher: *know thyself!*

Practical Consequences

What is Teresa telling us in these opening words? Basically, that to begin the way of prayer and reflection is the easiest thing in the world and that it involves a simple act of turning inwards and taking time to look at our own unique 'interior castle'. If we want to sum up her agenda it is based upon the fundamental question, *'Who am I?'*

We have begun by asking this question and have started to wonder if we are the person who seeks a

34

better status or a bigger bank balance, or if we are, in fact, someone other than this. This leads us to the other fundamental question of this opening: *'What do I really want?'*

In unravelling and exploring the answers to these two questions we will be drawn into the centre of ourselves, to the centre of our 'interior castle'.

Exercise Two

Drawing Your Castle

Set aside half an hour and find a quiet spot where you won't be disturbed. Have ready a large piece of paper and plenty of drawing materials such as crayons.

Make yourself comfortable and do some of the stillness exercises suggested in the Appendix.

When you are ready, ask yourself the question *What do I really want?* and scribble down all the answers that come to you. Do not be selective but accept whatever comes, even if it is disturbing or surprising. Repeat the process with the second question *Who am I, really, really?*

When this process has come to a natural end, take the large piece of paper and draw your 'castle'. The castle is you and this is your 'life map'. You may want it to be a series of concentric circles or spheres like Teresa's. Or you may prefer a different shape – or no shape at all.

The floor is open, be as imaginative as you like. You may want to use colours, symbols, shapes or patterns; whatever speaks to *you* and builds up a picture of *your* castle.

Now place as best as you can your answers to the two questions in your castle. You may want to place some answers at the centre, some on the edge. Take your time and let it happen.

Take a short break – have a cup of tea or a short walk.

Now come back to the picture and see what you think about it. Is it a good representation of how you see yourself? Have you missed something out? If you were to do it again would you change anything? Would you show it to your friends? If not, why not? And if so, which of your friends would you show it to and why?

Finally, to finish the exercise, imagine you're in the inn with Teresa and Fray Diego on that winter's night in 1579. Imagine you've just arrived, you're cold and hungry – but as you enter notice how warm and cosy it is. There may be music playing, nuns giggling in a side room, the publican just serving supper.

As you become accustomed to the sights, sounds and smells, look into the main parlour where you see two old friends chatting by a roaring fire. Study their features: the sturdy, middle-aged prioress, still beautiful and robust, full of life and laughter; the peaceful friar, sitting relaxed and reposed. Notice their clothes and the expressions on their faces. Listen to their conversation for a moment and notice the turns of phrase. You are becoming interested in what they're talking about. You overhear phrases: *'A crystal diamond'*, *'a maze'*, *'beautiful vision'*, *'serpents and lizards'*.

Finally you can contain your curiosity no longer –

go forward and introduce yourself. Notice how they react, look at the expressions on their faces and don't be surprised when they draw you into their conversation and pull up an extra chair for you. After you've talked with them a little while produce your castle picture and see how they react. Notice how you feel about their comments and whether you're pleased with them or not. Chat with them and see what observations they make.

When you are ready leave the conversation, thank them and return to the present to finish the exercise.

✳

The above exercise will produce different effects for different people. Try it and see. Note particularly how it affects your perceptions of yourself and where you place your spiritual life and God relationship within the context of your castle.

Chapter 3

The Second Mansion: Balance

'Peace, peace,' says the Lord, 'to you, my sisters.'
How often our Lord spoke words of peace to his
apostles. Believe me, if we do not possess peace
and strive for it within our own home, we shall
not find it in anywhere else.... Then even in this
life, you will enjoy such happiness, far more than
you could ever imagine or desire.[1]

The journey has begun and we have started the
process of praying. In this chapter we shall be
concentrating on the role of prayer in our lives.

For Teresa the second mansion is 'an extremely
dangerous state'. The soul has made a determined
decision to leave the life it had before but still does
not have the strength and knowledge to 'go it alone'.
It finds it difficult to cope with the stresses of the
'lizards and snakes':

> In some ways they suffer a great deal more than
> those in the First Mansion, though their danger is
> less, because they now understand the peril
> they're in.

At this vulnerable stage, it is extremely important to preserve a balanced rhythm of life that will
carry us along regardless of any inner turmoil. Most
religious communities and bodies through the ages
have placed special importance on such a 'rhythm of

38

life' and we shall look now at what that means in practical terms.

The Door to the Castle

Teresa says in the second mansion that 'the door into the castle is prayer'. What does she mean by prayer? Teresa is quite clear all along what she *doesn't* mean – a sort of cartoon abstraction from life. Throughout her life Teresa was a practical woman who lived fully in the cares and problems of her day. She couldn't have succeeded in the tasks she set out to do if she hadn't been well-organized and competent. As a contemplative nun, Teresa would have had to be practical, pragmatic and down to earth.

The key to most religious life is *balance* and when we embark upon the life of prayer it is important to be aware of this. The great founders of monasticism and monastic orders, such as St Benedict, have all stressed this and when we look at a document like St Benedict's *Rule*, the guide for living he prepared for his monks, we find a humane and balanced message for living.

Teresa, too, gives various tips and hints for a balanced life in *The Interior Castle* and in the second chapter she gathers together various pieces of practical advice.

Human Needs

Teresa would have found today's large cities very different from her sixteenth-century world. Yet human needs remain the same whatever the time or the culture. Part of my work is with a charity caring for homeless people. Anyone who lives or works in any large city will come into daily contact with this modern social catastrophe.

Through my work I realize more and more that there are basic human needs that have to be met if we are to live a fulfilled life. I would classify these into five categories: good food, good sleep, good relationships, good work and good prayer. The first four create the necessary conditions for the last, which in turn energizes the other four. Without all five of these requirements we do not function adequately. Let's look at each in turn and see how they interrelate.

Good Food

Our moods can be affected by our physical states. Gerard W. Hughes, a Jesuit priest, describes in his book *Walk to Jerusalem* how he would notice that when he arrived at a hostel, tired and hungry, the world seemed an awful place and undertaking the pilgrimage in the first place seemed a ridiculous waste of time. After a meal, a bath and a good night's sleep, the world did not seem so bad and many of the pressing and urgent problems of the previous night had disappeared. In our homelessness project, our first action with new arrivals is to offer them food and drink. Then we can investigate other needs such as housing and medical help.

Just so in the spiritual life: many spiritual directors attest to the wisdom of examining people's eating and sleeping habits before moving on to spiritual difficulties. Once someone is eating well and regularly many apparently spiritual problems simply disappear.

40

There is a famous story that some nuns one day discovered St Teresa in a kitchen devouring a roast partridge with her bare hands. The good sisters were shocked and asked Teresa what on earth she was doing. She replied: 'When I fast, I fast; and when I eat partridge, *I eat partridge.*'

There is something wholesome about the love of good food. St Benedict, for one, places great emphasis on the pattern and habits of eating:

> We consider it to be enough for the daily meal, whether at the sixth or the ninth hour, that there should always be served two cooked dishes, to allow for the weaknesses of different eaters; so that if someone cannot eat of the one dish he may still make a meal from the other. So two cooked dishes should be enough for all the brethren. And if fruit or tender vegetables are to be had, a third dish may be added.[2]

In the small communities of L'Arche, founded by Jean Vanier, where groups of adults with learning disabilities and assistants live together, great emphasis is placed on the importance of the meal time as an occasion where people come together and share each other's company. This happens in a simple way in ordinary homes, when food is presented well and there is a sense that the person who has prepared it presents it lovingly as a gift.

The Church itself places a meal at the centre of its celebrations of Christ's victory over death: the love feast of the Eucharist or Mass. Every day and in every country across the world, Christ's final meal with his followers is re-enacted in commemoration of that last night together, of friends gathering for one final time to share with their teacher and enjoy each other's company. This is part of the reason that Christians come together on a regular basis, to remind themselves that they are com-panions: literally, they 'share bread together'.

The importance of good, balanced eating is central to the spiritual journey and in our own times, when we are more concerned about what we eat and where it comes from, this makes good sense.

When Teresa begins to describe the more unusual and unexpected effects of deeper mystical prayer she is even more insistent on the need to preserve a good, balanced daily rhythm of eating and sleeping to guard against spurious or false spirituality. She has strong words on this subject:

Some women, because of long prayers, vigils, severe penances, or other physical weaknesses may have poor health. When they receive spir-itual consolation, the physical body can't take it and they are overcome. Interior joy makes them feel tired and weak and they drift into a sleep. They think this is 'spiritual sleep' because they suppose that the soul's state must match the state of the body, and they abandon themselves to a sort of stupor.... They fancy they are being carried away by rapture, but I call it being carried away with nonsense. They are simply wasting their time and ruining their health. ... The prioress should make sure that such a nun spends very few hours in prayer, and eats and sleeps well until she has regained any strength lost through lack of food and sleep.[3]

Good Sleep

Security and shelter are fundamental to our needs. Once we have provided our homeless clients with food and refreshment, we set about finding them somewhere to stay. Security and safety can be physical, in terms of a place to sleep; we might also be aware of mental or psychological security – a safe space where we can be ourselves. Many people in busy families shut themselves away for a short time each day in order to unwind a little. Much of Teresa's life was dedicated to creating a safe space where her sisters could live in security, tranquillity and peace as they pursued their journey towards God.

When we embark on our own spiritual journey it is important to set in place a regime of sleep, recreation and rest that will carry us through difficult periods. When we are feeling tired and distracted in prayer we should ask ourselves, 'Am I getting enough sleep?' It is surprising how many people who have advanced in prayer over several years often neglect this important aspect of their lives.

Listen to your body at all times – and especially listen to your tiredness.

Good Relationships

As human beings we need others. Donald Winnicott, a British psychotherapist, once said that there was no such thing as a baby existing on its own. From the moment we are conceived we are never alone; we are constantly surrounded by others and we define ourselves in relation to them. Indeed, there is a whole school of psychotherapy which devotes itself to looking at the nature and extent of these relationships – the 'object relations school'. In the words of another contemporary British therapist, Hymie Wyse, 'In the beginning was the group', which is to say that we find our true identity through interactions with the people around us.

For the balanced life it is important to ask ourselves what sort of relationships we have with others. Sometimes the people we live with do not nourish us and we find ourselves becoming distracted and uncomfortable. We should then question our surroundings and the company we keep.

Teresa emphasizes the importance for beginners to link up with others who are leading a spiritual life – not only with those who are at the same point in the journey but 'those who are in the rooms nearer the centre'.

So often, especially in the spiritual journey, we can convince ourselves that all is going well and that we don't need the advice and help of others. But perhaps we should follow the advice of St Ignatius, who recognized the need to 'talk seriously about serious things' and it may be beneficial to ask ourselves whether we have anyone in our lives who we can relate to in this way.

Good Work

For many people, unemployment means misery and lack of purpose, and even a life on the streets. Occupation does not necessarily mean having a paid nine-to-five job. It can be anything that brings meaning and fulfilment to our lives, such as raising a family, a political cause or an absorbing hobby. Teresa refers to 'good works', by which she means that part of the Christian tradition that places special emphasis on the need to be engaged fully in the daily struggle with existence that besets us all – especially the weakest and most vulnerable members of society.

As Christians we are, like Christ, called to radical social action and, like him, we will often be drawn into situations where our call for action leads us into conflict with authority. In a country such as India, with its great traditions of contemplative and mystical prayer, there can still be almost universal respect for a pragmatic Christian such as Mother Teresa, who embodied the Christian need to engage with the poorest and weakest in society, no matter how unattractive they must be. Those who follow the call of Christ must necessarily go one step further and ask, 'Who benefits from my work?'

In the midst of our work God is constantly calling us and we shall find as we enter deeper into the castle that spirituality and action become harder to distinguish from each other. At this stage, however, Teresa notes that God 'seeks us even when we are caught up with our own worldly affairs, business and pleasure, buying and selling'.[4]

Good Prayer

It could be argued that only when we have the above four areas of our life in order should we turn our attention to prayer. The reality, though, is that prayer is constantly with us and there is no artificial distinction between the above activities ending and prayer beginning.

One can make a distinction, however, between prayer and prayerfulness. Prayer happens in those discreet moments that we 'put aside' to engage in the 'activity' of prayer, whereas prayerfulness is a state of readiness and awareness of God's continued presence which can infuse our lives like a bundle of herbs in a stew.

There are, then, various general points about prayer that may be helpful to someone who is embarking upon this strange path for the first time.

Simplicity

The key to prayer is simplicity.[5] The old adage 'Pray as you can, not as you can't' holds a store of truth and, as Teresa demonstrates in her letters and writings, was a saying she would very much subscribe to. It is helpful to experiment with prayer: for instance, try praying in different places and at different times, employing new methods and techniques, but always bearing in mind the first principle of simplicity in all things. Simone Weil, the French mystic activist, called prayer 'attentiveness' and that is exactly what it is.

Routine

Remember the rules of balanced eating, sleeping and relationships; a certain amount of disciplined routine is also important with prayer. Edward Ford once wrote:

> Of all the things you can do for yourself, getting a job, going to school, working for charity – creative solitude on a daily or semi-daily basis (in brief, endurable chunks) will be the most important.[6]

Make a space and time each day for 'creative solitude' when you can be alone, to reflect on your life and listen to what God is saying. Some people have a special area: a shrine, a chapel or just a certain corner of a room, often with flowers, pictures or 'ikons' (holy representations in art). This may help you feel free to experiment. Alternatively you may be drawn to a 'sacred spot', such as a local church or place of natural beauty. Allow yourself to explore.

Time

A certain routine for times of prayer is important. Traditionally, the times often chosen for prayer are the 'hinges of the day': morning and evening. In Indian tradition these are seen as times of instability when light meets with dark and in the consequent encounter the voice of God can be heard more clearly. The Christian tradition of 'morning and evening prayer' is an established practice, especially in monastic communities, which goes back to the beginning of Christianity itself. In today's world, when so many of us are working during the day, the hours of morning and evening provide us with a welcome moment for reflection in an otherwise busy schedule.

How long should I pray for?

Well, how long is a piece of string? Some people need an hour every morning and evening, whereas others might find five minutes will do. You need to experiment and see what is best for you. Half an hour seems to feel right for many people and is often suggested as an appropriate time for those beginning a journey of prayer.

How do I keep the time?

Some people are quite happy to keep an eye on their watches. However if this is too distracting there are a variety of ingenious methods of keeping time. Some people I know use a kitchen timer set to buzz after half an hour – these have proved enormously popular in some monastic communities! Others record some relaxing music at the beginning and end of a thirty-minute tape, interspersed with a period of silence. A short piece of calming music leads them into prayer and brings them out of it. Once again, a little imagination goes a long way!

Place

As with time, so too the place we choose to pray in can be very important.

If we cultivate an atmosphere of 'prayerfulness' throughout our daily lives then it will become possible to listen to God in all the places of our daily lives: on the bus to work, in the marketplace, at home with our families and so on.

However, for the discreet 'prayer times' where we step out of our daily routine, it may be helpful to have a 'special place' to which we can return to seek peace and tranquillity. Many people find this in a church or chapel. However you may have a favourite place in nature to which you return.

You may want to adapt a part of your house or garden to act as a prayer shrine where you can spend your special time with God. Sacred pictures, flowers, candles, etc., may all help to establish the mood of this place.

Having a safe place to 'retreat' to for prayer often helps to establish a constant rhythm of prayer in our lives. As with time the space we use will depend upon what works for us. Remember: 'Pray as you can, not as you can't.'

Silence and Listening

We have found our place, we have made our time, what do we do now?

In simple terms we just listen. 'What?' you say. 'Is that it – isn't there anything more sophisticated?' The answer is 'No, not really.' If we assume that prayer is attentiveness to the voice of God, then we hear that voice by listening to the world around us, to others, and to our bodies.

The first word of St Benedict's *Rule* is 'Listen!' and it is the first rule of prayer. Simple though it sounds it is not so easy to put into practice and we can think of numerous occasions when we have failed to listen to someone else, or have not felt listened to ourselves.

Crucial to listening is the cultivation of silence, not only a silence without but a silence within. Of the souls in the second mansion, Teresa says they:

> ... can hear when the Lord calls them. As they slowly come closer to His Majesty's chamber, he becomes their good neighbour. God's mercy and goodness are such that he calls us constantly, no matter how much we fail him. He always calls us to draw near to him.[7]

We shall explore listening in greater depth later in one of the exercises.

Teresa writes that God's voice may be heard 'through the conversations of good people, or from sermons, or from reading good books, or in many other ways'.[8]

God speaks to us in so many ways that once we have begun to cultivate the art of silent watchfulness we will astound ourselves by the number of ways in which God communicates to us. As Teresa says, 'His call could come through sickness, trials, or the truths we learn when we are at prayer.'

The use of sacred scriptures and texts has always held a special place in the practice of prayer. Some texts may often appear outdated and irrelevant today as some people have difficulty with sexist or patriarchal language. For others the sheer barbarity of certain texts (such as parts of the psalms where the dashing of babies' heads on rocks is advocated) may be too much. To compensate for these more unattractive aspects there has to be set the sheer poetry and power of so many sacred texts.

Even when we have trouble with a certain text it is often a good idea to stay with the disturbance and pray through it. Staying with something uncomfortable and letting the reason for the discomfiture appear will often outweigh the initial problem.

The word of the Lord is indeed a 'two-edged sword' that 'cuts more finely than any human sword' and we may find that 'leaning up against the text' will reveal untold delights to us. It is a good idea to choose a short text and spend some time ruminating on it. The Benedictines have developed an art of using texts known as *Lectio Divina*. Read a short passage a few times over until a certain phrase speaks to you; when that phrase or word has rooted inside you, the book is closed and the meditation commences.

A spiritual director once advised me: 'Pop a text into your mouth and chew on it a little to let its flavour come out.' This is sound advice that will produce unexpected results.

Which text should I choose?

Consultation with a spiritual guide is useful, but if such a person is unavailable there are plenty of readily compiled daily readings obtainable from the religious section of most bookshops and libraries. It is surprising how often texts seem to 'find you' – I find increasingly that books are there when I need them most, or a friend will recommend something that turns out to be just what I needed. Coincidence? It has happened too many times now that I am convinced this is not so.

Spiritual Directors and Soul Friends

Who are these 'spiritual directors' I have been talking about? Some people prefer the title 'soul friend' (an old Celtic term), others use the term 'spiritual guide'. Whatever the title the intention is the same: we are seeking someone who we can meet on a regular basis in order to 'talk seriously about serious things'. Usually we would meet once a month and the space would be there to use as we considered best.

The spiritual director is *not* a counsellor. Counsellors or therapists are there to accompany the psychological process of healing, whereas spiritual directors are there to accompany travellers on their spiritual journeys – the real 'director' is the Holy Spirit. A spiritual guide should be well versed in a spiritual tradition and have the necessary time and

51

space to be at the disposal of the person seeing them. Spiritual direction is a very personal thing, and as with finding books that are helpful to us, there is an element of mystery about finding the right guide. There is a saying in India that 'when the student is ready the master appears' and this is often the case with spiritual direction. The guide will often help to serve as a balance to whatever may be occurring to the other person at that time, and often this balance is necessary to keep things in perspective. As with our example of the over-zealous nun, we are sometimes so caught up in ourselves (especially when it comes to spiritual matters) that we cannot 'see the wood for the trees', and when this happens our guide will be able to offer a sense of perspective.

Teresa, especially when she was receiving her 'mystical gifts' of voices and visions, could not decide whether or not the experiences were authentic, whether or not they were coming from a good source. Time and again she sought advice from spiritual directors, but not all this advice was beneficial and often there were problems with communication. Be that as it may she stresses the need to be obedient to such directors.

The word 'obedience' has its roots in the Latin words 'to listen with' – when we talk to a spiritual director we literally 'listen with' them to God's voice and hear what it is saying to both of us. Occasionally, however, the director and his pupil hear two different things, and then it is important that both remember that the real director is God and that the spiritual director is more like a midwife, facilitating by observation and care, rarely intervening but always supporting.

Other Techniques

As with any other field of human endeavour prayer is not immune to all the techniques, schools and methods that can be encountered elsewhere. Teresa offers insights and ways that many find useful, but hers is not the only way. Thus, as you become more involved with learning and reading about prayer you will gain an awareness of the many different techniques. Most are quite straightforward despite their fancy names.

Thus, 'savouring' the flavour of scriptures is, as we noted, often referred to as *Lectio Divina*. The imaginative contemplation we experienced at the end of the previous chapter is a form of *Ignatian Spirituality* which places special emphasis on uses of fantasy and imagination. We will study this method in more detail shortly, along with the practice of stillness known as *Stillness Meditation*, which can be found in Eastern and Western traditions. It may be accompanied by the repetition of a short phrase over and over again, such as 'Jesus Christ': this is often referred to as a 'mantra'. Whichever technique is used the overall aim is to foster the atmosphere of mindfulness and attentiveness, always listening to God's word.

During the course of this book we shall try practical exercises in most of these areas in order to illustrate the many areas of Teresa's teaching. In addition, you will find more information about these techniques in the books mentioned in the Bibliography.

Summary

We have entered the castle through the 'gate of prayer'. This is not in isolation from the rest of our life but communicates with and informs everything else we do. As we have seen from the words of wise teachers in the past, we are advised to seek balance in our rhythm of life if we are seeking fulfilment and happiness. Teresa advises us:

> At this stage you should not give a thought to spiritual consolations. That would be a very unworthy way to start building such a huge and precious castle. If you build on sand, the whole construction will soon fall down.[9]

Our only peace can be found within:

> What peace can we find anywhere if we can't find peace within ourselves? ... Believe me, if we do not possess peace and strive for it within our own home, we shall not find it in anywhere else.

Once we have attended to the five areas we have looked at here, and begun a regular and committed prayer life, we will have the necessary foundations in place to commence that search for deep inner peace.

Exercise Three

Listening

This exercise is based on the simplest of the prayer techniques mentioned above and can be performed in a simplified form at any time and at any place. It is essentially an exercise in listening.

Set aside half an hour, preferably at the beginning or the end of the day – at the unstable time when light meets dark.

Find a quiet spot, preferably somewhere where you won't be disturbed. It will probably be impossible to find somewhere completely silent, but the exercise works better if there is some background noise anyway. You should try to be in a place where you can hear something of the world outside.

Make yourself comfortable (whatever position you are in try to keep your back straight) and arrange that twenty minutes will pass without you having to look at your watch (set a kitchen timer or prepare a tape as previously described).

Now begin to listen, first to the most distant sounds: traffic, aeroplanes, birds, the wind, children playing and so on. Do not let your mind comment on these sounds, just accept them and let them pass.

Now move to the sounds in the room: the water pipes, a clock ticking, a neighbour's radio and so on. Again, don't comment on them – just listen.

Finally, listen to the sounds within yourself – your heart beating, your breath, the ringing in your ears. As each sound appears be aware of its presence, its beginning, middle and end. Notice how much sound we filter out and how much we do not even notice. As you go through the exercise be aware of the great hierarchy of sounds that enfold and surround you. Be aware of the great energy of the world around you – life everywhere!

If the exercise takes you to a place of stillness and quiet within you take the opportunity to 'listen' to God. What is God saying to you at this moment in your life? If you would like to go further, take an incident that has happened to you recently – say an argument, a great joy or blessing – and ask God to speak to you through it. Stick to the first incident that comes to mind, no matter how trivial and recall your reaction to the events at the time. Stay with it and let any messages it has for you speak to you.

When you are ready, return to the world of sounds by concentrating first on those close to you, then on those further and further from you until you are back in the world.

Spend a few moments evaluating the exercise – notice in particular what feelings it has evoked in you. Close with a short prayer of thanksgiving at the sheer wealth of sound that surrounds us.

*

Note: If your hearing is impaired or if this exercise presents physical difficulties, take some time to use stillness exercises to quiet the mind before listening to God through an incident in your life: use visualization if it helps. Listening is a state of mind as much as a physical attribute:

> Heard melodies are sweet,
> But those unheard are sweeter.
>
> Keats

Chapter 4

The Third Mansion:
Saying and Showing

And there was a man who came to him and asked, 'Master, what good deed must I do to possess eternal life?' Jesus said to him, 'Why do you ask me about what is good? There is one alone who is good. But if you wish to enter into life, keep the commandments.' He said, 'Which?' Jesus replied, 'You must not kill. You must not commit adultery. You must not steal. You must not bring false witness. Honour your father and mother, and you must love your neighbour as yourself.' The young man said to him, 'I have kept all these. What more do I need to do?' Jesus said, 'If you wish to be perfect, go and sell what you own and give the money to the poor, and you will have treasure in heaven; then come, follow me.' But when the young man heard these words he went away sad, for he was a man of great wealth.

Matthew 19:16–22

Teresa's third mansion can be seen as an extended meditation on this scripture passage from the New Testament. She refers to it several times and says of it:

Since I began to talk of these dwelling places, I have constantly thought of this young man because we are exactly like him.

57

These souls know that nothing would induce them to commit a sin, many would not even commit a venial sin inadvertently. They make good use of their life and wealth. They cannot, then, accept patiently that the door to the presence of our King is closed.[1]

It is worth spending a little time with this passage so that we can understand why it meant so much to Teresa at this stage of the journey.

A Guided Meditation

We have already mentioned the practice of what is called *Ignatian Guided Meditation*: this is the process of reading through a scripture passage, putting ourselves in the scene and then using our imagination to allow the passage to speak to depths of ourselves which have previously remained unexplored. It is worthwhile applying this process to the story of the rich young man and examining some of the elements within, as no doubt Teresa did when she was thinking of her third mansion.

First we should consider the rich man himself. What does he look like? What sort of clothes does he wear? (Armani? Versace?) Where does he live? What sort of car does he drive? (We don't have to confine ourselves to first-century Palestine here, in fact the more contemporary the image the better; the message of the Gospels and Christ is as relevant today as it was two thousand years ago.) Imagine his lifestyle, his friends, his job: he may be a barrister, an accountant, a stockbroker.

Use your fantasy and draw up a picture of this young man. Would you like him if you met him? Or would you want to run a mile? Perhaps you may want to talk to him – perhaps you may want to *be* him. Try it, put yourself in his position, imagine the clothes, the fast cars, the expensive restaurants, the busy working hours (if he works, that is).

Having met the rich young man we are now ready to introduce him to Christ. Imagine the scene for the meeting. Again, we have free range here – the Gospels are silent on the location so we can pick anywhere. It could be at a party, or in a public place. Christ could be preaching at a church, or holding a meeting somewhere. The Gospel passage describes how the rich young man came to Jesus, and so we can ask ourselves: 'Why does he want to see Jesus? What motivates him?' Place yourselves in his shoes for a moment and ask yourself, 'Why do I need to see this man? What is impelling me to seek out his advice?'

Having set the scene and spent some time watching Christ and how he speaks to the other people before he encounters the rich young man (again, notice Christ's appearance, his manner of dealing with people, tone of voice, etc.), we are now ready to witness the encounter between the two. Notice how the rich young man approaches Christ (and if we are imagining we actually are the rich young man, notice our feelings as we approach Christ, expectations, hopes, fears and so on). Allow the dialogue to unfold: *'Master, what good deed must I do to possess eternal life?'* Notice Christ's response: *'Why do you ask me about what is good? There is one alone who is good.'* Brusque and somewhat enigmatic, what can this mean? *'There is one alone who is good.'* Register the rich young man's reaction to this response. Register your own reaction to this response. Listen to Christ listing the commandments: *'Love your enemies, love your neighbours, love your partner, love your parents.'*

As he lists them note the feelings rising in the rich young man. Is he indignant, or bored? Does he feel Jesus is stating the obvious? *'I have kept all these. What more do I need to do?'*

Jesus' response? *'If you wish to be perfect, go and sell what you own and give the money to the poor, and you will have treasure in heaven; then come, follow me.'* Notice the rich young man's response – he is very sad and disappointed.

What has happened in this encounter? In a moment the feelings of self-sufficiency and pride have been wiped away, the rich young man leaves lonely and dejected.

If you are observing the scene in your mind you may perhaps want to ask Christ what is happening and why he is treating this obviously well intentioned young man so harshly. In many respects the rich young man has done everything right. He is a *good* man, he has led a decent and upstanding life and has probably helped a lot of people. He has 'kept the commandments' and done everything prescribed to him by society and probably by his parents too. Why then does he fall at this hurdle and why does Jesus seemingly treat him so harshly?

It is worth pondering this question as this is really the hub upon which the Gospels, Christianity and Teresa's *The Interior Castle* turn. Paraphrasing St Ignatius, the most difficult choices and decisions of our life are not between *the good* and *the bad*, but between *the good* and *the better*. This requires a greater skill of discernment and a greater attachment to what Teresa calls 'God's will'.

It is at this fine point of the soul that we can miss the subtle means of God's action moving us, gently and irresistibly, in ways we would perhaps rather not go if left to our own devices.

Christ says to Peter at the end of the Gospel of St John:

I tell you most solemnly,
when you were young
you put on your belt
and walked where you liked;
but when you grow old
you will stretch out your hands,
and somebody else will put a belt round you
and take you where you would rather not go.

John 21:18

Teresa's point in the third mansion is that if we pursue the call of God long enough there will come a point when we feel called to go in a direction 'we would rather not go'. For the rich young man this involved giving up what he held most dear in his life – his rich lifestyle. But for each of us it will be different.

Often it will be the thing that we love and value the most in our life, not just our possessions, but our loved ones, our children, even our own faculties or health. We will often fight tooth and nail to prevent this happening, yet it may be 'the one thing necessary' to bring us to God. The loss of something very close to us and the pain and suffering caused are themes throughout Teresa's journey and we shall explore them in greater depth later when we look at 'the dark night'.

For now, let us to return to our meditation and see what lessons we can find in it.

Saying and Showing

Close to the parable of the rich young man in St Matthew's Gospel is the parable of the two sons (note how Christ often gives his most profound teaching in the form of a 'parable' or good old-fashioned story):

'A man had two sons. He went and said to the first, 'My boy, you go and work in the vineyard today.' He answered, 'I will not go,' but afterwards thought better of it and went. The man then went and said the same thing to the second who answered, 'Certainly, sir,' but did not go. Which of the two did the father's will?' 'The first,' they said.

Jesus said to them, 'I tell you solemnly, tax collectors and prostitutes are making their way into the kingdom of God before you. For John came to you, a pattern of true righteousness, but you did not believe him, and yet the tax collectors and prostitutes did. Even after seeing that you refused to think better of it and believe in him.'

Matthew 21:28–32

As with the parable of the rich young man this parable is about actions and words, what we say and what we do. The Austrian philosopher Ludwig Wittgenstein once said that 'what cannot be said can be shown, and what cannot be shown can be said'.

In our journey into the interior castle of our being we reach points where we find we are on the edge of expression. Part of the difficulty of travelling the spiritual road is finding the right words for our experiences, if words there are.

In the following chapter we shall look at how Teresa uses metaphor, pictures and analogies to bridge that divide. Meanwhile, both parables we have been looking at highlight the gulf between word and deed. The rich young man claims to be a seeker of God, righteousness and truth, yet his actions reveal that he is not prepared to 'put his money where his mouth is' and act on the spiritual desires he feels. In the parable of the two sons this is more clearly shown where words and deeds contradict each other. At the end of the telling Jesus pushes the point home by directly comparing the son who acts rather than talks with the prostitutes and tax collectors – a daring comparison and as shocking today as it probably was then.

Teresa would agree with the dictum 'Act first, think later!' and states clearly:

God can only apportion the reward for us according to our love for him. This love, my daughters, must not be a fabrication of our imaginations, but must be proved by our works.[2]

Time and again Teresa emphasizes the need for good works and the need for our actions to be congruent with our desires. This she feels is particularly true for the 'professional religious', the priests and the nuns:

Believe me, it is not a question of whether we wear the religious habit or not; it is whether we practise the virtues and submit our will in everything to the will of God. The aim of our life must be to do what God requires of us.[3]

63

She also has strong words for those who through caution and self-restraint get stuck in these mansions and can make no further progress because their life is so well-regulated there is almost no room for God to act:

> The penance these people do is well-ordered and balanced, like their lives. They value their lives because they won't be fit to serve the Lord, which is right and proper, so they are very careful in their penances in order not to injure their health. You need never fear they will kill themselves – they are far too sensible! Their love cannot over-power their reason. If only it would![4]

In a world that is over-regulated in so many ways, a world run by computers and machines and by the clock, it is increasingly difficult for 'love to over-power reason'. Teresa's plea in this chapter is for a bit more recklessness in our lives, a little more of the passion that we have seen she possessed in such an abundance. She calls us to let go of some of our cares and let God be God. We are being called to the ecstasy of our true being.

Conclusion: 'The Rich Young Men Have You with You Always'

We have seen how at the end of the parable of the two sons Christ shocks us by remarking that the tax collectors and prostitutes are making their way into the kingdom of God before the high priests and virtuous. We can perhaps begin to see what he means by this now that we have explored together Teresa's interpretation of the parables.

In Teresa's schema it makes perfect sense. The high priests, the upright, the model citizens and the rich young men can proceed so far but no further. They will be stopped by their own efforts. There comes a point where God has to take over. This process has begun in this mansion but will burst forth in the next.

God works best in the poorest and weakest members of our society or the poorest and weakest parts of ourselves. Remember, each of us is as much a tax collector or a prostitute as we are rich young men and high priests. These all represent parts of ourselves.

Time and again the God of the Old and New Testaments reveals himself in deserts and waste-places, weakness and rejection. It is to our own desert places that God is calling us to pay attention.

The central teaching of Christ, the so-called 'Beatitudes', state:

How happy are the poor in spirit,
theirs is the kingdom of heaven.
Happy the gentle,
they shall have the earth for their heritage.
Happy those who mourn;
they shall be comforted.
Happy those who hunger and thirst for what is
    right;
they shall be satisfied.
Happy the merciful;
they shall have mercy shown them.
Happy the pure in heart;
they shall see God.
Happy the peacemakers;
they shall be called sons of God.

Happy those who are persecuted in the cause of
   right;
theirs is the kingdom of heaven. Matthew 5:3–10

All is contradiction here. The way of Christ is
indeed the way of paradox and our further explo-
rations will help us discover how Teresa navigates
us through the essential mystery of paradox which
is our deepest being.

Exercise Four

Inner Desert

*The third mansion has been called the Mansion of
Sincerity. We are called at this point in our journey
to sincerity with ourselves, and especially towards
our weak spots. We shall explore this in the following
exercise.*

Take the usual space and time to prepare yourself
for the exercise (half an hour in a reasonably
peaceful place where you won't be disturbed).

Having used some stillness exercises spend some
time contemplating your own desert within, the
parts of yourself that you most despise, are
ashamed of or would rather forget. You may like to
concentrate on an incident that happened where
you were ashamed of your behaviour or an aspect of
your character that you can't stand. Or you may
want to take one of the characters of this chapter –
the rich young man, the lazy son, the tax collector
or the high priest – and see how many of your bad
characteristics are in them. You may decide to talk
to some of these characters. Conversely you may
have a sense of your inner desert as a place, colour

or mood. Wander in it, look at it, experience its feel and touch — it may contain cacti or other prickly things.

When you are ready, take these 'desert qualities' to Christ. Imagine him as we pictured him in the rich young man meditation, either talking at a party, in a church or walking in an open place. Imagine yourself telling him how you feel about these unsavoury aspects of your self and *listen* to what he has to say about them.

Finish with a short prayer such as the 'Our Father' or a prayer for guidance to wholeness and healing.

✳

Note: Carl Jung, the twentieth-century psychotherapist, described the desert aspects of our self as 'the shadow': that part of ourselves that we keep in check but which can have a lot of power over us.

This exercise is about getting in touch with our shadow. It may be painful and difficult and you may want to talk with someone afterwards. A spiritual guide is always helpful, but a close friend is equally good.

Remember that Jung also said the shadow contains 'ninety per cent pure gold'.

Chapter 5

The Fourth Mansion:
On the Edge of Infinity

Now as I begin writing about the Fourth Mansion it is very necessary for me, as I've said, to commend myself to the Holy Spirit. I beg him to speak for me from now on, so that I may explain the issues clearly.

At this point onwards they begin to be super-natural and it will be most difficult to talk about them clearly, unless His Majesty undertakes it for me.[1]

As we enter Teresa's fourth mansion something strange has happened. The outline of the landscape seems to have altered subtly. There has been a shift in our outlook. It is as though 'all is changed, changed utterly'. Teresa says that this is the point where 'the natural and the supernatural combine and it is here that the devil can do the most harm'. For this is the point where our ego defences break down.

If in the third mansion we were still desperately clinging on to our images of ourselves, no matter how misguided, at this stage of the journey they begin to crumble away and something new begins to emerge. Teresa's powers of description become vivid and it is here that she shows her great skills as a poet, a mystic and a writer; her use of symbols and imagery is striking. We have discussed the castle, the journey, the lizards and so on, but now, as we approach the bounds of comprehension and meaningful discussion, new symbols and images appear which sometimes have a dream-like quality about them. It is to dreams we shall turn next.

The Mystery of Dreams

Our journey into the castle began with a vision or dream of the castle itself, glittering and hovering mysteriously over our thoughts. As Teresa reaches the edge of certainty and expression she relies increasingly upon imagery and pictures. It is as though words can no longer contain what we are experiencing and we need to 'show' rather than 'say'.

In our conscious daily life we spend most of our time 'saying' (or at least trying to say) rather than 'showing'; in our unconscious life the other part of our being may often spend more of its time 'showing' things to us rather than 'saying' them. One of the most striking and spectacular ways this happens is through dreams. Some people are inveterate dreamers, they come down to breakfast each morning with a fresh bundle of night-time adventures to relate. Others seem to go from year to year without ever having had a dream.

I have known people who have only ever had one or two dreams, yet their lives have been irrevocably altered by them – such was their power and importance. Since Freud, psychologists and psychotherapists have been increasingly fascinated by dreams and there are many theories as to their origin and meaning. From our point of view they are interesting in that they can often be a way for the unconscious, perhaps suppressed, spiritual side of ourselves to communicate a message to our suppressing conscious mind.

Jung recalls just such a dream in *Memories, Dreams, Reflections* which occurred at a time when he was having problems finding the way forward for his life:

I found myself in a dirty, sooty city. It was night, and winter, and dark, and raining. I was in Liverpool. With a number of Swiss – say half a dozen – I walked through the dark streets. It had the feeling that we were coming from the harbour, and that the real city was actually up above, on the cliffs. We climbed up there.

When we reached the plateau, we found a broad square dimly illuminated by street lights, into which many streets converged. The various quarters of the city were arranged radially around the square. In the centre was a round pool, and in the middle of it a small island. While everything around was obscured by rain, fog, smoke and dimly lit darkness, the little island blazed with sunlight. On it stood a single tree, a magnolia, in a shower of reddish blossoms. It was as though the tree stood in the sunlight and was at the same time the source of light.

My companions commented on the abominable weather, and obviously did not see the tree. They spoke of another Swiss who was living in Liverpool, and expressed surprise that he should have settled here.

I was carried away by the beauty of the flowering tree and the sunlit island, and thought, 'I know very well why he has settled here.' Then I awoke.[2]

The dream has a striking 'Teresian' quality: there seems to be a pattern that is not unlike that of the interior castle.

Thus, we have on the edges the darkness: the night, winter, rain, fog and smoke. We have the regular arrangement, the 'mandala', and at the centre we have the source of light and beauty just as in Teresa's description.

As Jung described his dream we may recall our own dreams; notice in particular how he recalls the temperature, the light, the other people with him, his reactions to events. The dream quite clearly has a message but it is often misleading to try to 'interpret' every dream. Jung does not 'interpret' the dream in a traditional sense but lets it show its message to him. He comments:

> This dream represented my situation at the time. I can still see the greyish-yellow raincoats, glistening with the wetness of the rain. Everything was extremely unpleasant, black and opaque – just as I felt then. But I had had a vision of unearthly beauty, and that was why I was able to live at all. Liverpool is the 'pool of life'. The 'liver', according to an old view, is the seat of life – that which 'makes to live'.
>
> This dream brought with it a sense of finality. I saw that here the goal had been revealed. One could not go beyond the centre. The centre is the goal, and everything is directed towards that centre.[3]

It was as though at this stage of his life Jung's unconscious was revealing a message that could only be communicated to him through symbols, colours, shapes and a certain amount of drama. This is often the case with dreams. It is not so much the specific details that are important as what they show in mood, colour, light and feeling.

'I saw water'

Our life, and all life, begins in water and it is the place we return to in dreams when we enter our deepest existence. It is notable that the Bible both begins and ends with scenes of water. At the very beginning 'God's spirit hovered over the waters' and breathes life; at the very end John sees an ecstatic vision of the New Jerusalem where from the throne of God 'the river of life flows crystal clear' on either side of which are the trees of life.

Christians undergo a rite of initiation into the faith called baptism. As the person is immersed in water they are reminded of the destruction and of the new life that water represents: it is the life-bringer but sometimes also the destroyer. In traditional language, at baptism 'we die with Christ'.

The imagery of water is irresistible and often in dreams we see images of rivers, streams, oceans – or perhaps more prosaic things like baths, swimming pools and pipes. Teresa, too, found herself irresistibly drawn to the element and declares in the fourth mansion:

> Water, for me, is the best illustration of spiritual things. I am so dull and stupid, but I love this element and have studied it more closely than anything else.[4]

One can imagine the importance of water in the

Spain of her day; even today, with increasing global warming, we ignore its value at our own risk. She had turned to the symbolism of water before in her earlier *Life*, where she explains how beginners to prayer must think of themselves as those

> ... setting out to make a garden in which the Lord is to take his delight, yet in soil most unfruitful and full of weeds. His Majesty uproots the weeds and will set good plants in their stead. Let us suppose that this is already done – that a soul has resolved to practise prayer and has already begun to do so. We have now, by God's help, like good gardeners, to make these plants grow, and to water them carefully, so that they may not perish, but may produce flowers which shall send forth great fragrance to give refreshment to this Lord of ours.[5]

At this point she introduces her famous analogy of the 'four waters':

> It seems to me that the garden can be watered in four ways: by taking the water from a well, which costs us great labour; or by a water-wheel and buckets, when the water is drawn by a windlass (I have sometimes drawn it in this way: it is less laborious than the other and gives more water); or, by a stream or a brook, which waters the ground much better, for it saturates it more thoroughly and there is less need to water it often, so that the gardener's labour is much less; or by heavy rain, when the Lord waters it with no labour of ours, a way incomparably better than any of those which have been described.[6]

We have begun the spiritual search 'under our own steam'. We have used all the spiritual buckets and pails and watering cans at our disposal to advance ourselves in the spiritual life. We have put into practice all the spiritual counsel such as we described previously.

However, as we proceed we find that we can do less and less by our own efforts and slowly, ever so slowly, God starts to take over. In *The Interior Castle* Teresa simplifies the analogy and sets before us just two types of water which lie in two basins:

> These two basins of water, then, are filled in different ways. One fills with water which flows into it from a distance, through a network of cleverly constructed conduits; the other is built near the source of the spring itself and fills noiselessly and effortlessly. If the water is abundant, as in this case we are speaking of, it overflows from the basin into a great stream that runs on without the aid of pipes and machinery. No aqueducts are needed, no human skill is required for the water flows continuously.[7]

The first basin, artificially filled, represents prayer that begins with the person and ends in God. The second, where the water wells up spontaneously and marvellously, is that which begins with God and ends in the person. Teresa calls the first 'active meditation' and associates it with the first three mansions of the castle, the second she terms the 'prayer of quiet' and it is the predominant activity of the final three mansions.

The fourth mansion represents the transition from one to the other: at this point we really do stand on the threshold of infinity.

The Flowers are Opening

In her *Life* Teresa describes this crucial stage thus:

> The understanding, at any rate, counts for nothing here; the soul would like to shout praises aloud, for it is in such a state that it cannot contain itself – a state of delectable disquiet. *Already the flowers are opening: see, they are beginning to send out their fragrance.*[8]

Teresa is very insistent that prayer should not be an end in itself but is a means to an end – that end being the glorification and praise of God, 'the flowers'. For Teresa, all authentic prayer ends in praise and the end to which we are created is the praise of God.

The second important thing to note in this passage is the lessening role that reason and thinking begin to play:

> I know no other terms in which to describe it or to explain it, nor does the soul, at such a time, know what to do: it knows not whether to speak or be silent, whether to laugh or to weep. This state is a glorious folly, a heavenly madness, in which true wisdom is acquired, and a mode of fruition in which the soul finds the greatest delight.[9]

At this stage, she counsels us, it is not so important 'to think a lot, as to love a lot'. Once this process begins the person

> should quietly and gently try to stop thoughts from wandering, but not seek to stifle imagina-

tion and freeze the mind. It's good for the mind to think that it is in God's presence and to consider who this God is. If, as it feels this, it is transported out of itself, that's good; but it should not try to understand what is happening within. It is a gift given to the will and the soul should be left to enjoy it in peace.[10]

Often in the spiritual journey, as we have seen above, there is a time for questioning, criticism and self-examination: this is not it. Now is the time for silence, quietening and waiting. The mind might be racing away trying to work out what is happening, but the will and heart are at peace: this is a clear sign to leave the mind to its own devices and follow the heart. How rarely we let ourselves do that today! In spiritual matters we need so much psychological or scientific explanation that we often cannot cope with the imperative just to be. And yet, try as it might, the mind cannot find an answer at this point. It has gone beyond questions and answers and must accept that God is in the driving seat from now on.

This is what Teresa means by 'loving more' and it is to tutor us to greater love that the rest of her account is dedicated.

'Unless a grain of wheat ...'

The fourth mansion is probably the most difficult mansion to write about. This is because Teresa is dealing with one of the most mysterious and important aspects of the spiritual life: the process of transformation.

How does transformation occur? How can something that was bad, destructive or diseased become something wholesome, life-giving and worthy? The answer is often beyond our capacity as human beings and lies close to the wellsprings of mystery.

Jung compared the processes of human transformation to the chemical processes of alchemy: the ancient art of chemical transformation that sought gold from dirt. Remember that Jung suggested that the shadow contained 'ninety per cent pure gold'. This can give us a clue as to where to look for transformation.

For Teresa, this can only happen when we 'let God be God', when we allow a greater force into our lives that transcends the limits of our small finite egos. 'Unless a grain of wheat falls on the ground and dies, it remains but a single grain – but if it dies it yields a rich harvest.'

As we move through the final three mansions of the castle we shall see what this dying to ego means and the implications it has for our lives.

Exercise Five

Dreaming

As we have mentioned above, dreams are a store-house of pictures and imagery. In this exercise we try to plug into this powerhouse and see what messages our unconscious is sending us.

Take the usual time and space to prepare yourself for the exercise: set aside half an hour in a quiet spot.

Once in a relaxed state recall a dream that has been important for you. It may be one you had recently, or one you had a long time ago. (It often helps to sleep with a notepad by the side of your bed if, like me, you easily forget dreams.) It is sometimes best to choose for this exercise the first dream that comes to mind, rather than pondering too long on which one to choose. If a dream spontaneously comes to mind there is usually a reason why that is so. Now, go through the dream once again, particularly noting the mood, colour, light and feeling. It may help to write down this information.

Once you have recalled the dream it is now time to enter it: choose one of the characters in the dream (or if there are no characters choose an animal, plant or other object) and narrate the dream from that character's perspective. It is helpful to note especially how you, the dreamer, are described. What observations has the character to make about you?

Once you have finished with one character, move on to another, or perhaps an object, an animal or plant. You may want to dialogue with the different parts. As you do so try not to intellectualize too much but allow the process to develop as freely as possible.

When you have finished this exercise ask yourself what the dream has shown you. You may like to repeat the process with the same dream or another at a later stage. You may prefer to take anything that comes up to Teresa to chat with her about it – she may have some useful insights!

Finally, take your insights to Christ as we imagined him in the previous exercise. See what his comments are.

＊

Most of our exercises can profitably be carried out either alone or in pairs. The dream exercise in particular works very well in pairs: often the process of retelling a dream to another person reveals aspects of it that may lie dormant when we investigate it alone.

Chapter 6

The Fifth Mansion:
The Little Butterfly

A Government Health Warning

From now to the end of *The Interior Castle* Teresa is concerned with describing the perils and delights of the union of the soul with God. After the fourth mansion of transformation we are entering a different world, we are indeed 'on the edge of infinity'.

However it would be foolish to think it is all plain sailing from now on. Far from it. As Teresa stresses time and time again, the devil and our own destructive powers are as active as ever. Throughout the journey humility has been essential and from now on it becomes imperative. Teresa is constantly showing us ways we can be on our guard against false spiritual pride, and we shall look at these later.

We are now presented with a new difficulty, that of description. Who has access to these rooms – and how do we know if we have entered them? If we have attained union with God, then what are we doing wandering around here on earth, doing the shopping, going for a walk or having a nap in the afternoon? Surely this world is not a suitable place for such enlightened beings?

Again Teresa is aware of this problem and suggests, especially as we approach the final mansions of union, that we receive 'glimpses' of these states whilst on earth even though we may not be able to live them fully here. When talking about Teresa's mansions with groups there sometimes creeps in a sort of spiritual prize-day mentality: 'Oh, which mansion are you at then?' 'I'm definitely in the fourth mansion, I left the third ages ago.' Yet nothing could be further from the spirit of Teresa's writings. She is always at pains to point out that the seven mansions are merely a rough guide and that

> although I have mentioned only seven mansions, each one contains several rooms: above, below, around it, fair gardens, corridors, fountains and much else to delight you.[1]

The book is meant to assist the journey, not the other way round; in so far as Teresa's descriptions help they should be welcomed, and in so far as they hinder they should be disregarded (as she herself counsels). She provides us with a structure as a means to explain and talk about the spiritual journey: it is up to us to make of that structure what we will.

Having said that, Teresa says at the beginning of the fifth mansion that 'there are really very few who do not go into these mansions. Some get farther in, others less far, but most manage at least to enter.'[2]

This is a comforting thought as Teresa tells us the fifth mansion contains many 'riches, treasures and delights' which are almost beyond description. Ever resourceful she introduces another picture or metaphor to help carry us across into the final parts of the castle: the little butterfly.

81

The Power of Words

The origin of words is fascinating and when we look at the roots of some of our common words we will be amazed to find how ancient they are: many go back to Greek and Roman times, some even beyond that to the ancient languages of the first peoples of Europe.

Take, for example, the word '*soul*'. This, like the German word *Seele* comes from the Gothic *saiwala* and the old German *saiwalô* and, as Jung pointed out, these can be connected with the Greek word *aiolos*: mobile, coloured, iridescent. When we use words such as *psychology*, *psychotherapy* and *psyche* we are drawing on the ancient Greek word *psûkhé*: this important word means breath (say it softly – '*souk – hey*' – and you will notice that you gently draw breath in and then exhale); it also refers to the Greek goddess of that name, '*Psyche*' as she is normally referred to in English. The legend attached to her is fascinating and involves a mysterious midnight encounter with *eros* who we mentioned at the beginning of the book. There is also an episode where she is carried up by *Zephyrus*, the god of the winds. Also, the Greek word *psûkhé* means *butterfly*.

Thus, these two words '*psyche*' and '*soul*' have attached around them a cluster of meanings and moods: bright, coloured, iridescent, moving, breath, life, spirit – all somehow condensed in the image of the butterfly. I must admit to having always been fascinated by these fragile creatures. There is something slightly miraculous about their appearance, which Herman Hesse, the German poet, sums up so precisely in his beautiful poem *Butterflies in Late Summer*:

The time of many butterflies has come,
In late phlox scent, dreamily rolls their dance.
Silently they come, swimming out the blue:
The tortoiseshell, the admiral, the swallowtail,
The purple emperor and fritillary,
The shy hairstreak and tiger-bear.

Expensively dressed, in pearls and satin;
Glittering in jewels, they sway before us.
Splendid and sad, silent and dazed;
Strangers here, bedecked in the honeydew
Of the under-meadows they have left in paradise.
Short-lived guests from the East,
That we in dreams, forgotten homeland, see,
Receiving their pledge of a more perfect world.

Symbols of everything beautiful and fleeting,
All that is too gentle and overwhelming.
Melancholic and gold-dressed guests
At the old summer-king's last feast.[3]

I remember as a child watching the big, dark red
admirals and peacocks hovering over the rotting
plums and pears at the bottom of our garden on
still, late summer days in September and feeling
something similar to the mood Hesse evokes in his
poem: that of wonder at these 'short-lived guests
from the East'. They really are potent symbols of
the unconscious.

In later years the butterfly image has often
returned (especially in dreams) and it is one I
cherish and draw strength from. At the end of this
chapter we will explore ways in which we can draw
on these potent symbols of transformation. For
Teresa, too, the butterfly was a potent symbol which

she uses to describe the mysteries of the fifth mansion.

The Silkworm and the Butterfly

In the fifth mansion the butterfly represents the whole process of spiritual change, and Teresa tells a story which highlights the need for *preparedness* in the spiritual journey:

> To explain this more clearly, I'll use an appropriate comparison. This will also show how, though this work is performed by the Lord and we can do nothing to make His Majesty grant us this favour, yet we can do a great deal to prepare ourselves to receive it.
>
> You have heard of the wonderful way in which silk is made, a way nobody but God could conceive. You have heard how it comes from tiny eggs, like peppercorn seeds. I only know of this second-hand, for I've not seen it for myself, so any inaccuracy will not be mine. When the mulberry tree springs into leaf in warm weather the tiny egg, which had been quite lifeless, begins to live. The caterpillar feeds on the mulberry leaves until it is fully grown. Then people put down small twigs upon which the silkworm instinctively spins silk from its tiny mouth. It forms a narrow cocoon of silk into which it buries itself. Then, instead of this large, ugly worm out of the cocoon there comes a lovely little white butterfly.[4]

For Teresa this is the story of the soul in search of God. At the beginning of our journey through the castle the soul awakened to begin its journey to its true self. Like the tiny silkworm eggs in the warm weather, it 'germinated so that the tiny caterpillar emerged'.

This was the moment of our first question: *'Who am I, really, really?'* The tiny grub is hungry for enlightenment and stuffs itself on all the books, sermons, talks and courses it can find (including reading books such as this one!). Today, when there are so many courses, retreats and workshops available it is easy to do this and one often meets people who are like these caterpillars moving from one course to the next, voraciously eating their way through all the spiritual nourishment they can get. (I must confess I do this with spiritual books and often find I can get a form of spiritual indigestion through them!) Eventually there comes a point when the caterpillar can eat no more – it feels nauseous and has no more appetite.

We reached this stage at the end of the third mansion, having done all we could on our own to improve spiritually and then finding it impossible to make any more progress. We began to experience the 'glass ceiling' of our own efforts and realized that there is a natural limit to what we can achieve by ourselves. It is now that the seeker will, in Teresa's terms, 'begin to spin silk and to build the house in which it must die'; which is to say, we must concentrate on the act of preparedness for God's action on us, rather than our action on God.

This chrysalis or transformation stage is the most difficult to describe. Although it begins in the fourth mansion it can extend throughout the remaining mansions, only reaching fulfilment in the union of the seventh mansion. It is mysterious and invisible and will almost certainly incorporate the encounter of the 'dark night' – a process we shall look at later. John Welch, an American Carmelite, has written a beautiful book, *Spiritual Pilgrims*, exploring the symbols and themes of Teresa's approach and comparing them with Jung's ideas. In his wonderful account of the transformation process he says:

> Freeing oneself for a relationship with God produces a container for transformation. The relationship is the container, the cocoon, which allows for deep contact between the soul and God. The union with God in the inner depths is experienced as a liberation, and the butterfly-soul emerges.[5]

In Teresa's words:

> His Majesty himself becomes the Mansion. When I speak of God being our Mansion and say that we ourselves build the home and dwell in it, it may seem as though I'm saying that we can add to what God does or take away from what he does. What we can do, however, is add to or take away from ourselves, just like the tiny silkworm. The little we can do is insignificant; it's really nothing at all, and so it will scarcely have been finished when God in his greatness unites us to himself.[6]

These are deep matters and once again Teresa is on the edge of language and expression. Here she is revealing the very end of the process (no less than the very end of life itself); the union of the soul with God – the 'mystical marriage' that we shall return to in the final chapter.

Here she expresses it as the cocoon of the ego

becoming Christ as the recreated soul emerges as the 'little white butterfly':

> All I've said comes to a climax here. As soon as the soul, by prayer, becomes entirely dead to the world, out it flies like a lovely little white butterfly! Oh, how great God is!
>
> The truth is that the soul does not even know itself the difference is so great; it is as great as that between the ugly worm and the white butterfly! It doesn't know how it could have gained so great a blessing.[7]

Welch comments on this passage:

> The development of the personality demands the re-enactment, over and over, of the story of the death of the worm and the birth of the butterfly. Our passages, crises, transformations all involve a dying and a rising. Teresa's *Interior Castle* is the story of one large transformation, one grand passage, one great initiation. The castle itself is the cocoon-container of a death and a new life. Each of the dwelling places marks varieties of transitions and turning points.[8]

We are destined as human beings constantly to reshape ourselves and constantly to be reshaped. John Henry Newman said that to grow is to change and to be perfect is to have changed often. The wonder of Teresa's little book is that she shows us how we can change and allow ourselves to be changed by the gentle guiding hand of a power greater than ourselves. Only in such change can we find salvation.

Exercise Six

Symbols of Transformation

As we have discovered, the butterfly is a powerful symbol of transformation which echoes across cultures and times. This exercise may evoke similar symbols and you may wish to investigate them further in the literature mentioned at the end of the book.

Take the usual time and space to prepare yourself for the exercise. A pen and paper, drawing materials or crayons may be useful.

Having taken some time to relax, imagine something (it may be an animal, a plant or a rock) to represent how you feel at this period of your life. Don't be too selective and preferably choose the first thing that comes to mind.

Let yourself be that thing for a moment. Notice how it feels when you are that thing. Notice if you feel different or if your mood changes. Do you have a voice? Can you make a sound? What sound do you make? What would you say if you had a voice? Notice where you can feel this creature or thing in your body. Does it inhabit one part of your body in particular?

When you are ready, open your eyes and write a short statement from the point of view of that thing of about one hundred words. Start each sentence with 'I ...' and address it all from the first person singular ('I am a lizard, I live under a rock and I have sharp spines to protect myself').
You may like to draw your creature.

When you have finished your statement, take a break and then come back to see how you feel about being that creature. Is there a message here? As with the previous exercise, it may be helpful to talk it over with a companion afterwards – perhaps you may want to read out the statement to another person.

✳

Some of the symbols this exercise produces may have many layers of meaning – don't stick to one meaning but let the symbol speak for itself.

Chapter 7

The Sixth Mansion:
Visions in the Night

O Guiding Night!
O Night more lovely than the dawn! [1]

In the previous mansion we glimpsed the first delights of the new life that awaits us as God slowly takes over in our lives. We saw how Teresa symbolized this by the emergence of 'the little butterfly'.

However, our journey has by no means ended and there is much more to come – especially trials. In fact, the trials that await us may be far worse than anything we have experienced up to now and may put the attacks and taunts of the lizards and devils of the earlier mansions into shadow by comparison.

The sixth mansion is a time of great trial and danger. Teresa takes the dangers seriously and accordingly writes more about the sixth mansion than any other. In it she methodically goes through the new experiences the soul receives and presents some guidelines to help to discern if we are on the right path.

Chief amongst the trials is what has been termed 'the dark night': that is, a total collapse of meaning and hope that can throw the spiritual seeker completely off course.

Although the little butterfly of our true self has emerged, Teresa says:

> This little butterfly has not been more quiet and tranquil in its life and yet you should see how restless it is! May God be praised! It doesn't know where to settle. By comparison with what it has experienced everything on earth leaves it dissatisfied, especially when God again and again gives it this wine, which at every taste brings some new blessing ...
>
> It was once fearful about doing penance, but now it is strong. It once clung to the bonds of relationship, friendship or possessions. It could not break free. All its resolutions, acts of will and desires seemed only to tie it more firmly. But now it is grieved at having to fulfil its obligations in case it should in any way be led to disobey God. *It grows tired of everything, for it realizes that no creature on earth will give it true rest.*[2]

The old self is breaking down and falling away, together with its old ways of attachment and relating – but the new mode of existence isn't in place yet. The soul is somehow living between two worlds.

No one is more misunderstood than the person who embarks on the spiritual journey, and the trials Teresa talks about, are probably just as true today as they were 400 years ago.

The image of a spiritual seeker, seen as standing outside convention and society is, of course, an old and venerable one, common to many traditions. One thinks immediately of the *sadhus* – wandering holy men of India – who after a life as householders and

responsible citizens leave their homes and families
and set out upon the spiritual search far from home.

Not just men, of course. Mira, a well-loved mystic-
wanderer happened to be a contemporary of
Teresa's (she lived from 1498–1550), and like Teresa
she sings poems of the difficulties of one who has
renounced worldly things for the spiritual search:

Binding my ankles with silver
I danced –
people in town called me crazy.
She'll ruin the clan,
said my mother-in-law,
and the prince
had a cup of venom delivered.
I laughed as I drank it.
Can't they see? –
body and mind aren't something to lose,
Krishna has already seized them.
Mira's lord can lift mountains,
he is her refuge.[3]

As we saw in the opening chapter Teresa was a
source of gossip, attacks and misunderstandings
about her spiritual practices and it must have upset
her dearly:

Those she thought were her friends desert her,
saying the most bitter things about her: they take
it to heart that her soul is ruined and that she is
quite clearly deluded and that this is the work of
the devil. They say that she will share the fate of
this or that person who was also ruined with
them. They say she's deceiving her confessors and
actually go and tell them this, giving stories of
similar cases where people were ruined and they
make endless derogatory remarks.[4]

92

Teresa counsels perseverance and tolerance in these conditions and actually feels they will be beneficial in instilling greater humility in the soul. They help concentrate the soul on the task at hand and remind us of the fundamental question we began with: *Who am I – really, really?*

While all this is going on, however, the seeker may experience more disturbing trials.

'The Spooky Stuff'[5]

Teresa's name is often associated with the 'spooky' happenings she used to experience: there are numerous accounts, from herself and others, of the visions, 'locutions' (hearing voices) and, most spectacularly of all, the flights and levitations. It is difficult for us, who live in a more scientific and sceptical age, to know what to make of these occurrences. And yet there is no doubt, as extensive research has shown, that these phenomena do occur and have outward manifestations.

Having encountered similar phenomena (although not quite as extreme as Teresa's) in my own work in the area of spirituality, I find Teresa's instructions and guidelines on dealing with these occurrences down-to-earth, full of common sense and extremely wise. She is more interested in concentrating on the practical implications of these events rather than metaphysical or scientific investigation into their origins. She is more likely to ask, *'How did you feel after the event?'* or *'What effect did it have on you?'* rather than *'Why did that happen?'* or *'Where do these things come from?'*

The main events she concentrates on are *locutions*, *wordless prayer*, *'the flight of the spirit'*, *visions* and *other sensory phenomena*. We shall look briefly at each in turn.

Locutions

As with all the supernatural phenomena, Teresa suggests it is better at the beginning 'to resist these communications', for 'if they come from God this is the best way of obtaining more, for when discouraged they increase'.[6] This is good, solid advice. If they continue she suggests some guidelines by which we can distinguish genuine locutions from false ones. She states it is irrelevant whether we perceive them as coming from inside, outside or elsewhere. What matters is the *effect* they have upon us and how we deal with them.

The first characteristic of a true locution is its strength and sincerity, which is joined to the second characteristic: the ability of a message to bring a sense of peace, comfort and lightness to the listener:

> Take an example: a person is afraid and troubled because her confessor and others tell her that her soul is under the influence of the devil. Then she hears a single voice saying: *'It is I, be not afraid.'* Immediately her fear leaves her and she is filled with comfort, so much so she believes that her new-found confidence can never be shaken.[7]

This persisting sense of peace is a good sign and suggests an authentic voice from the centre. Such communications 'do not fade from the memory, but remain there for a long time; sometimes they are never forgotten'. They are usually unexpected and have the character of something we had not expected to hear. They are quick and spontaneous, and do not have the character of something carefully and painstakingly constructed.

Finally, a single word is able to 'engulf a depth of meaning'. A single phrase or sentence may have a power and resonance out of all proportion to its size: 'These communications, in a manner I cannot explain, very often give us to understand more than is implied by their words themselves.'

Any locution, series of words or advice received in prayer should be treated with the utmost caution and perhaps a degree of disregard. For if the advice is from an authentic source then it will be repeated. If it is of such a power and quality as to convince us of its authentic origins, we should look at it from all angles to discover the qualities of strength, wholesomeness and spontaneity. If it satisfies these conditions Teresa would then suggest talking it over with a trusted advisor to get a second opinion. Finally, if all these stages have been followed we should have 'tested the spirits' sufficiently to dispel any doubt from our minds.

What are these 'locutions'? The locution is a voice from the deepest part of our being, rising and emerging to give some advice that our conscious ego has somehow mislaid. Teresa's method of approach to these phenomena, eminently practical whilst never dismissive and always open to new experiences, is typical of her and is characteristic of how she approaches the other spiritual phenomena of the sixth mansion.

Wordless Prayer

In Teresa's famous 'ecstasies' she would often go

beyond words into a region where wordless prayer alone was sufficient. At different times she calls these moments *ecstasies*, *raptures* or *transports*:

> When God intends to take the soul to himself, he removes the powers of speech. Though other faculties may be retained longer, here no word can be uttered. Sometimes the person is immediately deprived of all senses. The hands and body may become cold as if the soul had flown; there are times, too, when breathing seems to have stopped ...
>
> This supreme ecstasy only ever lasts a moment. But when it is over, the will is left so overjoyed and the mind is so transported out of itself that for a day or several days after the person is incapable of attending to anything but what excites the will to love God.[8]

These wordless, 'out-of-body' experiences seem similar to those experienced by latter-day charismatic and Pentecostal Christians. I remember once having to give a talk to a group of quite radical charismatic Christians on Teresa and feeling slightly nervous that they might find her writings too removed and isolated from their experience. I was pleasantly surprised when they listened to the account of the phenomena of the sixth mansion with great interest and then proceeded to confirm and explain details from Teresa's account. I felt as if I was getting an on-the-spot report of some of the occurrences she describes!

Phenomena such as the 'Toronto Blessing' and 'speaking in tongues' have made such 'supernatural' dimensions to prayer much more common today than they have been for centuries. Again, when we are asked to give advice and guidance in dealing with these spiritual manifestations Teresa's counsel can be invaluable.

The Flight of the Spirit

This is perhaps the most mystifying of all the phenomena Teresa describes. From her account it is difficult to distinguish whether she is talking about actual physical levitation or just the feeling of levitation:

> Here the soul suddenly feels such a rapid sense of motion that the spirit seems to carry it away with an alarming speed, especially at first.... Now it is powerfully snatched up despite its opposition. So the soul stops resisting, unable to do more than a straw drawn irresistibly by amber.... The Spirit raises our spirits with the powerful ease of the giant whose muscles would effortlessly lift a straw.[9]

From her description we have the sense of a great power operating and of being swept up by a force greater than ourselves. To illustrate her point she returns to the analogy of the waters:

> It seems that the cistern of water of which I previously spoke, was at first quietly filled in stillness. But now the springs once restrained by God, who limits the ocean's boundaries, are opened up and the streams flood into the cistern. The rushing mighty waves flow powerfully enough to raise high the little vessel of our soul. The ship and the pilot are unable to stem the tide. The fury of the

waters carries the ship along at its will. Even less is the soul able to choose where it anchors or bring its senses and faculties to aid control. He who holds them in his power gives the orders and all exterior aid is useless.[10]

This powerful description seems very apt for the whole process of the sixth mansion: it is the feeling of being carried away, of losing control, of God being in the driving seat. It is similar to the accounts of ecstasy in Eastern disciplines such as Sufism.

In India there is a tradition of talking of the seven 'chakras' of the body: these are seven points where bodily and spiritual energy are concentrated. They are located at the base of the spine, over the spleen, over the navel, over the heart, in the throat, in the forehead and on the crown of the head. The meditator concentrates on each area and allows energy to flow as freely as possible between the seven. Any blocks in energy-flow will lead to dis-ease, discomfort and stress. As I read Teresa's descriptions of the ecstasies they seem more and more like the descriptions of chakras being unblocked and energy flowing once again in the body.

In recent years in the West we have become more and more accustomed to seeing the body, mind and spirit as one organic whole and we have returned to the sensible view that health in one area can only come about through integration of the health of the other two.

Thus, our bodily health influences our spiritual health and so on (hence our insistence in the second mansion on a good, sound and balanced rhythm of life). I suspect that in the sixth mansion parts of the body-mind-spirit continuum that have been neglected in our lives will now begin to reassert their presence, perhaps in a surprising, forceful and dramatic fashion. We may be taken unawares by the power of these forces and Teresa, ever practical, stresses the importance of daily routine as being especially important during this time.

It is conceivable that in prayer we can experience phenomena that feel like the 'flights of the spirit' described by Teresa. As for experiencing actual levitation itself, I would prefer to 'pass over in silence of what we cannot speak'.

Visions

Teresa spends some time discussing visions as she was quite used to experiencing them.

She is, as before, strict in her criteria for acceptance of the veracity of visions and has strong words for those whose claims she feels are not authentic:

> Not just a few but several people have discussed this subject with me. I know by experience that what some have seen are figments of the imagination produced by overactive minds or vivid imaginations. There may be other reasons of which I am not aware, but those folk are so absorbed by their own ideas, feel certain they see whatever their imagination wishes. If they really had a genuine vision from God they would recognize it without mistake. But instead, such people put together, piece by piece, their own fabrications. In these no after-effects are produced on the mind, which is less moved to devotion than is evoked by the sight of a religious painting.
>
> Such fanciful ideas should be ignored as

mere fleeting dreams which pass swifter than
memory ... [11]

As with the locutions, she counsels that we examine
the after-effects of the visions: do they leave us in a
state of peace and joy, or do they depress and
disturb us? Also, we should not ask for them or
court them – we should let them come of their own
accord and accept them when they come. Finally, we
should discuss them with a trusted spiritual
director or friend who can offer an objective
perspective.

As with the locutions, these visions arise from
deep parts of the unconscious of which we had been
hitherto unaware – perhaps there is a connection
here with the dreamscape we explored in the
previous chapter.

Other Sensory Phenomena

The above four happenings by no means exhaust
the range and type of occurrences that Teresa
suggests we will experience at this stage. We can
receive experiences in any sense or dimension and
there seems to be no area in which God cannot act
at this stage. Thus we can have a peculiar sensation
of a delicious smell filling the air:

> There are other ways in which our Lord wakes
> the soul. For example, a person may be overtaken
> by a delightful zeal when reciting set prayers; one
> is surrounded by a fragrance so powerful that it
> infiltrates every sense. [12]

Teresa obviously had a keenly developed sense of
smell and she often uses descriptions of smells and

perfumes when trying to express a point in her writings. It is perhaps appropriate that, when she lay on her death bed, the other sisters noted a beautiful smell of fresh roses filling the house.

As well as sensations of smell, we may have bodily sensations of warmth, cold, comfort and discomfort. We may cry a great deal – Teresa gives a whole section to a discussion of this: it is often referred to as 'the gift of tears' and is considered a sign of great blessing in many traditions (St Ignatius, amongst others, was very prone to this gift).

Finally, we may become conscious of God in our presence, even though we don't see, hear or touch him – Teresa calls this an 'intellectual vision: don't ask me why'. It is a sort of sense of God's presence that is beyond the five senses.

With all this going on it seems 'the little butterfly' is very disturbed and cannot find rest – it sounds more like a marketplace experience than a desert experience! In view of all this Teresa counsels that we remain vigilant and clear, staying close at all times to the guidelines she has laid out for assessing the authenticity or otherwise of all supernatural occurrences.

Peace of Mind

To sum up, then, we have seen how as we deepen our spiritual search we can encounter some very strange phenomena. We can be thrown off balance by our own experiences – especially when they involve sensory perceptions such as seeing, hearing and feeling. Teresa constantly reminds us to be vigilant and to use common-sense, whilst never forgetting the need for a good daily routine of healthy eating, sleeping, relating, working and praying. She offers plenty of good advice should we experience any 'supernatural' phenomena.

Visions, locutions and tears are superfluous in themselves and the effects they produce on our lives are far more important than the events themselves. Accordingly, we should notice what effect they have on us and whether they are tending towards a greater peace and openness or disturbance and closedness. If the latter, although they may not necessarily be destructive, we should exercise caution and seek advice or a second opinion.

All true spiritual phenomena should lead to a greater sense of humility in the person who receives them. Any visions or locutions that tend towards a greater sense of pride ('I must be so special if God has blessed me with this wonderful vision') are suspect. One should never ask for these experiences and should accept them as part of God's gift, not something to be taken for granted.

All authentic spiritual experiences should lead towards a greater awareness of others and their difficulties. Teresa gives a wonderful account of the penitent who is so humble when in prayer but aggrieved when out of it:

> I smile when I see some souls who, when at prayer, think they would be gladly willing to be humbled and publicly insulted for God's sake, and

then shortly afterwards try to hide even their smallest fault. And to see them unjustly accused for a fault ... God deliver us from their outcry then! [13]

All our praying, all our searching, all our crying is for one purpose: in Bach's words, 'For the greater glory of God, and that my neighbour may be benefited thereby.' If we forget this we have gone horribly astray.

We are dealing with very powerful energies here – if we begin to use them to serve the ego and for self-aggrandizement then we are moving in a very destructive direction. This process of being 'thrown apart' is rightly called in the Christian tradition 'dia-bolic'.

All authentic spiritual experiences should lead to a greater concentration and awareness of God. This is Teresa's message within the tradition of the Roman Catholicism of her day, but this does not lessen the importance of that message for all people and for all times. As the old saying goes: 'Nowhere is God without witnesses.' As Christians today we have much to learn from the witness of God held in the experiences in all Christian denominations and all faiths. Accordingly, one should perhaps question spiritualities and approaches that close us to the experience of God in other people's lives, whether they are Christian or not: fundamentalism has no place in authentic spirituality.

As we approach these deeper levels Teresa re-emphasizes the importance of sound spiritual direction: we should find a sound and wise guide.

Time and again she urges us: 'Be perfectly open and straightforward with your confessor in recounting your prayer. Unless you do that I cannot be sure you will be safe or led by God.'

For Teresa, the confessor stands for Christ. 'It should be as if we were standing before Christ himself where we wished him to know not only our thoughts but everything relating to ourselves however small.'[14] In an age when counselling and therapy is so commonplace, there is a natural tendency to confuse them with spiritual direction. The spiritual director has a specific task which is not that of a counsellor or therapist: it is to help clarify the action of God in the life of those seeking guidance. To this end the only spiritual director is the Holy Spirit and the two people in the guidance session are listening in on what the Holy Spirit has to say. They listen with each other – they are 'obedient' to each other.

Teresa frequently urges us to concentrate on Christ's humanity:

> Some souls feel they cannot meditate on Christ's Passion, and even less on the most blessed Virgin or the saints whose lives strengthen and help us. I cannot imagine what such folk are to meditate on. Because it is impossible to withdraw one's thoughts from all bodily things, like angelic spirits whose beings are always inflamed by love. That is impossible for us while we remain mortal.[15]

She couples this with advice on avoiding too much disembodied 'prayer of quiet':

There are souls who start, advance half way and experience the prayer of quiet, tasting the sweet comforts God gives. Then they think they should enjoy these pleasures continually. I've said this before: they should stop giving themselves up to this absorption so much.[16]

The urge to leave the body behind and go off on a disembodied trip unencumbered with the sordid necessities of bodily existence has a long and venerable tradition as a favourite heresy in Christianity. It is known by different names, such as Gnosticism, Manicheism or Catharism, but it has always had the same message. Today we find it again in many new religious cults (the solar temple cult who committed ritualistic mass suicide at the advent of Comet Hale-Bopp, for instance) and it seems to represent a deep human aspiration to leave the mess of the body behind and fly off to the stars. Teresa is adamant that it is just this sort of temptation that we should constantly be on our guard against. For her, the constant reminder of the humanity of Christ and his Mother are vital in this respect.

Finally, in all these occurrences it is vital to keep a sense of humour! Once we start taking ourselves too seriously we will find ourselves in difficulties. As Thomas More said: 'The devil is a proud spirit, and cannot abide being mocked!' Teresa retains a lively and witty sense of humour throughout her account of some of the deepest and most sublime experiences a person can live through. In this respect she is an example to us all.

We cannot leave the sixth mansion without saying something about the 'dark night'. Towards the end of this part of our journey Teresa tells how 'the little butterfly'

> feels a strange loneliness. She can find no friendship on earth, nor any in heaven, apart from her Beloved. Meanwhile all companionship on earth is torture to her. Like one suspended in mid-air, she can neither rise up to heaven nor come down to earth. She is unable to reach the water though parched with thirst, a thirst that is unbearable. Nothing can quench that thirst and it will only be quenched by the water of which our Lord spoke to the Samaritan woman; but this she is not granted.[17]

What is happening here, and what do we mean by this phrase *'the dark night'*? It is, of course, Teresa's close friend St John of the Cross whose name is most closely associated with this phenomenon and his work, *The Dark Night of the Soul,* presents a masterly analysis of the phenomenon.

Iain Matthew, in his excellent book, *The Impact of God*, begins: 'John of the Cross speaks to people who feel unable to change.'[18] For the dark affects us at the point where we feel most impregnable or where we are most likely to resist the action of God. As the thing which is stopping God's full action in us may be very dear to us, the process may be extremely painful as it is part of an on-going purification which is often not completed in our lifetime.

This darkness might come from an internal

event, such as a crisis of faith; or it may be external, such as the death of a loved one or the collapse of a business enterprise. Thomas Green, who has written extensively on the dark night,[19] when asked how long it will last answers half-jokingly: 'That all depends on how much longer you expect to live.' By this he is suggesting that 'our life of prayer is really only the beginning of eternal life, and that the transformation God is working in us is truly the foundation of an eternity of loving him'.[20]

In Catholic tradition there is the notion that at death most souls will enter 'purgatory': a period of purgation and purification that will last until the soul is ready to enter completely into God's company.

It is John's contention that the experience of the dark night is the beginning of this purification process here on earth:

> Being purged here on earth in the same manner as there, since this purgation is that which would have to be accomplished there. And thus the soul that passes through this either enters not that place (that is, purgatory) at all, or tarries there but for a very short time.[21]

We are not talking here about a passing bad afternoon or an occasional depression, but rather a complete collapse of meaning and sense of disorientation. Constance Fitzgerald, an American Carmelite, describes it beautifully in her article, 'Desolation as Dark Night':

> Nothing makes any sense. The mind, while full on one level of a lifetime of knowledge, is in total

darkness on another, the level of meaning. We feel as if we had been duped, and succumb to silence, afraid to shock others by the depth of our cynicism and unbelief.... Memories do not mean what we thought they did. The memory is indeed empty, possessing nothing but the scattered remains of cherished experiences and the crushing remembrance of personal failure and defeat. This kind of clarity about one's miseries generates the overwhelming feeling of being rejected and abandoned not only by one's friends but particularly by God....

In fact, abandonment and the betrayal of trust are the hallmarks of this dark experience.[22]

The experience usually has this sense of ultimate crisis – of collapse of all hope, all meaning in life. It is accompanied by a sense of dryness in all things religious and an inability to find delight in prayer and contemplation. Whereas before we would happily spend hours in prayer which had a lightness and brightness about it, we now find even the shortest prayer painful and tedious. This type of crisis can be brought on either by an inner change, or prompted by an outer one – the death of a loved one or the loss of a cherished possession such as a house. Whatever the outward prompt, it activates a deep inner sense of meaninglessness and hopelessness.

It is important, however, to distinguish the dark night experience from a bout of depression, mental illness or neurosis. Part of John's genius is to lay down guidelines (a little like Teresa's guidelines for distinguishing authentic supernatural phenomena) for distinguishing the spiritual purgation of the dark night from darkness due to 'some bad humour or indisposition of the body'.

The first of these signs is: 'That as these souls do not get satisfaction or consolation from the things of God, they do not get any out of creatures either.' [23]

In other words, as well as not getting any satisfaction from spiritual matters, we also do not find consolation in going to parties, going out shopping or to the movies. We just find ourselves becoming increasingly ill-at-ease and out of sorts, which suggests that the malaise is not simply coming from a desire to return to more 'worldly' pursuits.

The second sign is: 'The memory ordinarily turns to God solicitously and with painful care, and the soul thinks it is not serving God but turning back, because it is aware of this distaste for the things of God.' [24]

The person is worried that they have lost God. Many things may have been lost or the cause of worry, but the one that causes most anxiety is that God has gone and will never speak to them again.

The cry of the soul is that of the lover in John's *The Spiritual Canticle*:

Where have you hidden,
Beloved, and left me moaning?
You fled like the stag
After wounding me;
I went out calling for You, and You were gone.[25]

The third sign is:

The powerlessness, in spite of one's efforts, to meditate and make use of the imagination, the interior sense, as was one's previous custom. At this time God does not communicate Himself through the senses as He did before, by means of discursive analysis and synthesis of ideas, but begins to communicate Himself through pure spirit by an act of simple contemplation, in which there is no discursive succession of thought.'[26]

Whereas before we may have been used to a prayer that used many words or clear images, we now find increasingly that we can no longer sustain this and our prayer and meditation becomes increasingly that of silent contemplation.

The dark night, then, has these three qualities: a sense of dissatisfaction with all created things, an anxiety that God has gone forever, and a move from structured discourse with God to a more direct experience of formless prayer. In addition, John suggests, the dark night has a quality of change-lessness about it – it doesn't have the feel of a mood or phase that will pass, but of permanence: 'return is not possible'.

We have entered on a phase of our development from which there is no return. In John's beautiful phrase: *'To come to what you know not you must go by a way where you know not.'*

On a recent visit to England, William Johnston, an Irish Jesuit who has studied with Zen monks in Japan and who is an expert on John of the Cross, was asked: *'When is the darkness dark enough?'* After some amusement amongst his listeners he reminded us that John says: 'O Night more lovely than the dawn! O beautiful night!' before adding 'Of course he wrote that when he was no longer having the experience!' The dark night can be a truly terrifying experience, and when it is the real thing it will stretch its recipient to the very limits of human comprehension.

Why does God allow this to happen? Iain Matthew, as perceptive as ever, suggests:

> If night first tells us that there is somewhere to go, it also announces that we cannot get there on our own. 'Night' presents suffering, not as the only place, but as a privileged place of God's inflow. In it, love not only comes; love also opens a space for its coming. That is the God-content of pain: it has power to unlock us at the point we cannot unlock ourselves.... Healing comes particularly in situations that take us out of our own control, in the kind of pain that is bewildering.' [27]

In the words of one of the Church's antiphons for Advent: 'What you have opened, no one can close; What you have closed, no one can open.'

The dark night is the experience that will finally open us to eternal life. It is perhaps the most dramatic and devastating of the spiritual manifestations of the sixth mansion: yet, if these writers are to be believed, it is the greatest gift that God can bestow on us (although it may not seem like that at the time) as it is his special way of preparing us for eternal life with him and him alone.

Summary

This has been quite a heavy chapter to get through and we have had to deal with many new experi-

111

ences. Teresa spends more time on this mansion than on any other. We have discussed each phenomenon in turn in order to understand fully that although the highest spiritual gifts may be experienced they contain the potential for the most 'diabolic' misinterpretation. As long as we stay clearly with Teresa's and John's guidelines, however, we should be able to avoid these.

The other reason for the danger here is that we are no longer in control; or at least the old ego, which has been our trusted guide (and sometimes our worst enemy), is becoming increasingly redundant. A new self is emerging which shares some of the features of the old person, but in other respects is radically different. The butterfly has a body and similarities with the caterpillar – but it no longer eats leaves and it now lives in the free air.

The changes we are describing in this book may take a lifetime to achieve. By reading about them in Teresa's account, however, we may be prepared to accept and recognize them when and if they do occur.

Exercise Seven

Energy Flow

In this exercise we spend some time acquainting ourselves with the seven energy centres: the chakras.

Take the usual time and space to prepare yourself. For this exercise it helps to be as still and undisturbed as possible. You will also need to be in a position where your back is straight – either on a straight-backed chair, or better, cross-legged or in the 'lotus' position. Many people cannot achieve a full lotus position, so a half-lotus is fine.

We will be using the exercise to briefly acquaint ourselves with the seven chakras. As there is a whole body of learning around this practice this will necessarily be very superficial; if you would like to explore the chakras in greater depth then it would be wisest to find a teacher experienced in the techniques. Begin by closing your eyes and becoming aware of your breathing. Be aware of the cool air entering and the warm air leaving the body.

Having observed the breath for a few minutes move first to the Root Chakra located at the base of the spine. Concentrate on this spot and note the quality and feel of the energy. The yogic practitioners talk of a 'coiled snake' resting here. It is a very powerful spot with a great deal of energy. Perhaps you associate a colour or shape with this spot – note it in your mind before moving on.

The Spleen Chakra is located between the Root Chakra and the navel and is close to the genitals, kidneys and urinary area. Once again, notice the feel of the energy here and see if you associate it with a particular colour or form.

Now move to the Navel Chakra. This is located two fingers below the navel and is again a source of great energy. When we say we 'have a gut feeling' about something we are referring to the energy from this chakra. It is an important seat of wisdom.

Next comes the Heart Chakra: the seat of the emotions and love. It lies above the heart and mediates the energy from below with that above.

Now to the Throat Chakra. This is the point where words and wordlessness meet. It is the moment of transition from the realm of non-expression to expression. It also connects the head with the body and the mind with the body, and so has to manage a great deal of stress when the two are not in harmony. Again, notice its shape and feel – it may also have a sound (as may the previous chakras).

The Forehead Chakra or third eye comes next. It is a centre of great wisdom and has great mental clarity. What do you see from it?

Finally comes the Crown Chakra. This is located on the very top of the head and it is as though a thread connects you with the ceiling or the sky above. It is where we make contact with the spiritual and our energy flows to God – allow the energy to flow towards God.

When you have covered each chakra, no matter how superficially or deeply, return to your breathing before opening your eyes again. You may like to draw or write down some of the experiences you felt at each centre.

*

Note: Of all the exercises this will be the most unpredictable. If you find that the exercise is producing unpleasant effects then return to the previous chakra or terminate the exercise – it's obviously not for you! This sort of exercise is best done under guidance, but even without guidance it may be useful in unblocking energy that has become caught up somewhere. I have personally found it an extremely useful and invaluable exercise and hope that you will have a similar experience with it.

Chapter 8

The Seventh Mansion:
The Mystical Marriage

*I have come so that you may have life: and have it
to the full!*   John 10:10

By the time we reach the seventh mansion we are
presented with something of a problem: we are
attempting to describe the indescribable. We may
puzzle at someone still being on earth, having
achieved the state of union implied by the seventh
mansion; surely this is the proper state of heaven?

Obviously there have been 'living saints' in the
history of humankind, but as we read through
Teresa's account of the seventh mansion this is not
what she has in mind. Her end point, her goal, is
not for a religious elite but is open to all: she seems
to imply that we *all* have the seventh mansion
within us from the beginning, and that by self-
discipline and the grace of God we can all enter into
it. She herself stands at the threshold of the
mansion in fear and trembling and feels that even
she will be unable to say anything about it:

O great God, a wretched creature such as I should
tremble at the thought of speaking on such a
subject. It is way beyond anything I deserve to
understand. Indeed, I have been in a state of
confusion wondering if it would be better for me

to finish writing just a few words about this last mansion I am to describe, in case people imagine I am talking about my personal experience. I am overcome with shame because, knowing myself, I realize what an enormous task I have before me.[1]

The difficulty Teresa is having here is in finding words to describe our basic nature as human beings.

We began our journey by asking two fundamental questions: *'Who am I, really, really?'* and *'What do I really want?'* These questions are answered in the seventh mansion: however the answer will come not in saying but in showing. From now on actions will speak louder than words. Therefore, Teresa ends the book with a call to action, or 'battle royal' in her words. Before reaching that point, however, she attempts a description of the state of the seventh mansion through her favourite means – metaphor.

The Mystical Marriage

There is a sense of completion, peace and calm lying over the final chapters of *The Interior Castle*. In Teresa's words: 'The little butterfly has died with the greatest of joy because she has finally found rest.'

After the transformation of the middle mansions we had the turbulence, the agony and the ecstasies of the fifth and sixth mansions. That has come to an end now, 'the soul now does not go into ecstasies, except on rare occasions'. Instead, we have entered the bridal chamber – the mystical marriage is being consummated.

All through her writings Teresa has made use of

116

the metaphor of sexual love to describe the soul's longing for God. This, of course, has a long and noble tradition in religious writing, going back to the *Song of Songs* in the Old Testament:

I am my Beloved's,
and his desire is for me.
Come, my Beloved,
let us go to the fields.
We will spend the night in the villages,
and in the morning we will go to the vineyards.
We will see if the vines are budding,
if their blossoms are opening,
if the pomegranate trees are in flower.
Then I shall give you
the gift of my love....

His left arm is under my head
and his right embraces me.
I charge you,
daughters of Jerusalem,
not to stir my love, nor rouse it,
until it please to awake.

Song of Songs 7:10–8:4

The language of the *Song of Songs* may be a little strong for some, but if we ignore this rich tradition in spiritual writing then we are in danger of ending up with a very impoverished view of God's richness.

It is hardly surprising that mystics, caught up in the rapture of God's embrace, should employ this language to describe their experiences of the union of the soul with God. Through it the divine becomes powerfully human and the human is made powerfully divine.

117

The powerful image of the Lord as divine flute player is also used by Teresa and helps to bring together the experiences of the mansions we have travelled through. As we approach the centre of the castle we have a strange sense of the inner peace of the union of the soul with God existing side by side with the turmoil of the outer mansions we have passed through – the cares and problems and anxieties that we had to transcend to get to this central point.

It is only now, as we reach the point of union, that we can begin to look back and see that those dark things are all parts of us and have all contributed to our completion as human beings. Teresa describes how in the centre the soul lies at peace in the marriage bed with God:

> God places the soul within the mansion of himself which is in the very centre of the soul. It is said that the empyreal heavens, where God dwells, do not turn with the rest of things: so the usual movement of the imagination and faculties does not seem to occur in any way that harms or disturbs the soul's peace.[2]

Away from the centre the soul remains able to return to the world and 'fight battles', safe in the knowledge that her lover lies waiting for her back in the bridal chamber:

> Our Lord occasionally leaves it to its natural weakness. The venomous creatures from the castle precincts and the moat all then seem to combine to revenge themselves for the time they were deprived of their power. This lasts briefly, it

118

is true, a day or a bit longer. But this disturbance, which arises from some passing event, helps the soul to learn just what benefits it receives from the divine company. Our Lord gives such strength and courage that they never desert his service, they do not go back on their good resolutions.[3]

It is as though the soul, having had a profound and total felt experience of the true nature of God within can no longer go back. Having realized its true nature, even though it must live in the confusion and chaos of the world, it can never go back on this and will remain united with God on its deepest level. Whatever disasters befall the self on the outside of the castle walls it will always, from now on, recognize the sound of the divine flute player from within its centre:

> Let's imagine that the senses and faculties, which I earlier compared to the inhabitants of the castle, have run away and joined forces with the enemy outside. After months and years of absence, they see their enormous loss and return to the castle precincts. But they cannot enter; their evil habits are difficult to throw off. Still, they are no longer traitors and they wander about just outside the castle. The King, holding court within, sees their good intentions and in his great mercy wants them to return to him. He, the good shepherd, plays upon his pipe with great sweetness and gentleness. At first they scarcely hear the call, but the shepherd teaches them to recognize his voice and to wander no longer, but like lost sheep to return to the mansions. The shepherd's power over his sheep is so strong that they

leave behind their worldly cares, which led them astray, and re-enter the castle.[4]

Martha and Mary

Finally, as we begin to look back at the journey and see where we have travelled, we have a sense of completion and wholeness. There are the outer walls, in touch with the world and assailed by troubles and cares; the middle mansions, full of change and wonder; and now, finally, the central mansions with their peace and harmony. It seems we can only find peace when we recognize our split existence: we are beings who exist in the world with all its cares, but who also have the potential to touch the divine and infinite in our hearts and minds. If there is one message in *The Interior Castle* it is that by living creatively the tension between the two we become fully human, fully alive.

To illustrate this point Teresa uses the story of Martha and Mary from St Luke's Gospel, traditionally used to illustrate the difference between the contemplative and active callings:

In the course of their journey he came to a village, and a woman named Martha welcomed him into her house. She had a sister called Mary, who sat down at the Lord's feet and listened to him speaking. Now Martha, who was distracted with all the serving said, 'Lord, do you not care that my sister is leaving me to do the serving all by myself? Please tell her to help me.' But the Lord answered: 'Martha, Martha,' he said, 'you worry and fret about so many things, and yet few are needed, indeed only one. It is Mary who has

chosen the better part; it is not to be taken from
her.'   Luke 10:38–42

As with our earlier contemplations, such as the rich
young man, this passage responds well to the same
imaginative treatment. See the action, see Martha
busy in the kitchen, surrounded by steam and pots
and pans. Perhaps she occasionally comes into the
living room to lay some knives and forks on the
table in a demonstrative fashion as if to say *I do
need some help, you know – this dinner doesn't cook
itself*.

See Mary, sitting on a scatter-cushion engaged in
deep conversation with Christ. She may have a
drink in her hand or be offering Christ a small bowl
of nibbles before dinner. Mary is the woman who,
just before Christ's crucifixion, pours the expensive
perfume, nard, on his feet and wipes it off with her
hair, much to the dismay of some of the assembled
company. She is obviously a woman of character
and strong dramatic sense: imagine how she is
dressed, how she talks – imagine that hair!

And in the centre of this, between these two
women so unlike each other, sits Christ. What is he
doing? How does he look? Where is his attention
concentrated? He is obviously aware of the situation
and when Martha finally explodes: *'Lord, my sister
is leaving me to do all the serving – please tell her to
get off her behind and help me!'* he is ready with his
wonderful answer: *'Martha, Martha, you worry and
fret about so many things, and yet few are needed,
indeed only one.'* What a wonderful, gentle reminder
to the over-busy and over-active!

Sometimes it seems that today we are more busy
than ever – our world is often a treadmill of activity:

working, looking after families, socializing, shopping, cooking. It goes on and on, almost without a break. And yet if we don't stop we will collapse in a heap – our bodies are just unable to cope with that amount of focussed activity.

On a recent visit to England the Dalai Lama remarked that when he sees our way of living in the West it seems to him like the mechanism of a watch (he is a skilled watchmaker so this analogy comes as no surprise): all the parts are carefully and precisely arranged so that each moves exactly how much and how little it is prescribed. Similarly, with our time schedules and daily routines, we are so hemmed in with commitments, arrangements and meetings that we hardly ever have the chance to stop and just 'be', the most difficult thing of all.

A traditional way of achieving this in the Christian tradition is what is known as a 'retreat'. This is a period of time set aside, often (but not necessarily) in a house in the countryside, where one is free to pray, meditate, wander and enjoy what has been called 'holy leisure'.

Many people are increasingly beginning to see how important these periods of 'time out' are and there is a growing retreat movement. There is even an annual guide published now which lists all the places of retreat available (see Bibliography).

Teresa, of course, is constantly aware of the need for contemplation, yet at no stage, especially in these final chapters of *The Interior Castle*, does she forget the crucial importance of the need to nourish our active, practical side. Teresa, as we saw in her life story, lived both fully and heartily and if we want to derive a *Rhythm of Life* based upon Teresa's writing then it will be first and foremost this: the integration and incorporation of the practical and the spiritual in our lives. She puts it thus:

> Both Martha and Mary must honour our Lord, invite him to be their guest and give him food. How can Mary do this while at the feet of Jesus, if her sister does not help?[5]

The Water is For the Flowers

To sum up, then: Teresa is adamant, as the journey comes to a close, that we have not received these spiritual gifts and blessings for our own personal use. On the contrary, 'the water is for the flowers' and the purpose of these insights has been to enable us to go back to the world around us, able to engage in the struggle of God's creation, confident that in our innermost selves we are united with the Lord in his bridal chamber:

> Perhaps you think I am talking about beginners and that one may rest later on. But, I've told you, this rest that comes to such souls is within them. Outwardly, they have less and they do not wish for it. Why do you think the soul sends from within its centre such desires, those messages I spoke of earlier? Why send them to those who dwell in the castle precincts and surrounding areas? To send them all off to sleep? *No, no, no!* The soul now engages in battle royal more fierce than ever to keep the powers of the senses of the entire body from becoming idle.[6]

Finally, then:

> So, sisters, be careful to lay a firm foundation.
> Seek to be the least of all and a servant to others.
> Look for ways to help others for it will benefit
> you more than them. If you build on this strong
> rock, your castle will never be a ruin. I insist and
> repeat: your foundation must not consist of
> prayer and contemplation alone; unless you make
> progress with the virtues and put them into
> practice you will remain dwarfs. And may it
> please God that nothing worse than making no
> progress overtakes you. You know that to stop is
> to go back. If you love, you will never be content
> with standing still.[7]

Thus the seventh mansion ends with a call to
action. In our final chapter we shall see what
implications this has for our day-to-day living, our
rhythm of life.

Exercise Eight

Martha and Mary

Take the usual time and space to prepare for the
meditation.

Once you are ready read carefully through the
Martha and Mary passage again. When you have
finished, spend some time imagining the characters: concentrate particularly on what they look like
and how they behave.

Allow the passage to be enacted in your imagination. Imagine the dialogues, see the expressions on
people's faces.

When you have gone through the scene, repeat it but this time place yourself in the position of Mary. Notice how it feels to be Mary: what music do you like, what do you like to eat and what do you like to talk about? How do you feel about Martha? What would you like to say to her? How do you feel about Christ and what he has said to you and Martha? What would you like to say to him?

Now repeat the scene as Martha. Again, ask yourself what you like to do on your night off. What's your favourite TV programme? What do you like to wear? How do you feel about Mary? Perhaps you may want to have a dialogue with her. Finally, what's your feeling about Christ? What do you have to say to him?

When you have finished close with a short prayer and take a break.

Reflect now on the experience and see where you felt most comfortable. Did you prefer to be Mary or Martha? Perhaps you preferred to be neither. What about the other person – did they irritate you or stimulate you.

Reflect on your attitudes to these two basic life-types: the contemplative and the active. How did Christ respond to you? What did you have to say about his comments?

*

This exercise should help stimulate some reflection on the two sides of life we have been discussing: the contemplative and the active. Modern psychology stresses the importance of differing personality types. Personality type indicators, such as the Myers-Briggs Personality Indicators, allow us an insight into these types and their interactions. As we deepen our awareness of ourselves we will see that we contain both types within ourselves; one may be more dominant than the other. Harmony often comes about through greater integration of the two.

This exercise could be acted out by two people or more, changing roles as appropriate – you will be surprised how powerful it can be when done like this!

Epilogue

Back to Life, Back to Reality

We have come to the end of our journey but we find ourselves where we began: rooted in the everyday world of practicalities and pressure, confusion and challenges.

However, everything is changed – we have arrived where we started but now we seem to know it for the very first time. We began our journey in the confusion and turmoil of sixteenth-century Spain, we end with our own lives now, at the end of the twentieth century awaiting a new millennium; yet the two worlds are not so very far apart. When we see the death of the old side by side with the emergence of the new then we cannot but feel nervous. Once we have completed Teresa's inner journey, however, we can return to the world of turmoil and confusion knowing that within we always have the indwelling presence of God to guide us.

In a final coda called *In His Service*, Teresa writes:

> When you have learnt how to enjoy this castle you will always find rest, no matter how painful your trials are, for the hope of returning to your Lord no one can stop. Though I have mentioned only seven mansions, each one contains several rooms: above, below, around it, fair gardens, corridors, fountains and much else to delight you. The

rooms have so much that you will wish to give yourself over to praise the great God who created your soul in his own image and likeness.[2]

For many years the writings of mystics such as Teresa have been ignored or concealed. Even in the churches few have had the time and inclination to discover their riches. In many respects the teachings of the mystics have been one of the best kept secrets of the contemplative and enclosed orders in the churches. These orders, such as the Carmelites, the Benedictines, the Jesuits, the Dominicans and the Franciscans have kept the flame of inspiration of their founders alive and have preserved their wise teachings over the centuries.

In the materially developed countries of the world today there is quite clearly a widespread thirst for the water of spirituality. Never before have we had such a materially advanced standard of living, and never before, so it seems, has there been such an emptiness at the heart of existence and a need for spiritual joy. This has been coupled with a widespread turning away from the doctrines and practices of the institutional churches. People seem less and less able to find their spiritual hunger satisfied in the practices of the mainstream churches. Perhaps the writings of the mystics will present a way forward for us all and the worldly wisdom of a gentle guide such as Teresa will enable a renaissance of spiritual belief and practice.

Today we can already see this happening; while the old wood dies new shoots are already springing up in the shade. In London we have groups such as the World Community for Christian Meditation, founded by an English Benedictine, Dom John Main and now run by his successor, Dom Laurence Freeman. It promotes meditation and the practice of contemplation amongst a wide and diverse group across the world.

Dom Laurence talks of a 'monastery without walls' and a 'monk without walls'. To be contemplative in Teresa's day it was necessary to withdraw to the fastness of a stone convent or monastery. Who's to say, with our modern communications and technical accomplishments, that Dom Laurence's vision will not become increasingly common: a monk without walls, a nun without enclosure.

Perhaps we are not witnessing the death of religious life after all, but the gentle growth of a whole new way of living inspired by the Holy Spirit. Talking recently about our rapidly dying century the philosopher Isaiah Berlin said: 'I have lived through most of the twentieth century without, I must add, suffering personal hardship. I remember it only as the most terrible century in Western history.' [3]

In the fifth century, as the all-powerful Roman Empire collapsed, a young Roman scholar, Benedict of Nursia, turned his back on the dying civilization and fled to the hills to cultivate a way of life that preserved peace and harmony while all around was in chaos.

As Teresa's gentle way slowly unfolds before us, like Benedict, we will find ourselves increasingly able to find inner peace and tranquillity, thus enabling us to cope with the demands the world makes upon us. We shall discover that our essential nature is, as the Sanskrit seers discovered four thousand years ago, *being – consciousness – bliss (sat – chit – ananda)*. Teresa's way is the way of

129

ecstasy, the way of being, the way of consciousness and the way of bliss.

If this book manages to make this gentle way a little better known to a wider public then it will have achieved its purpose.

This, then, is what I pray, kneeling before the Father, from whom every family, whether spiritual or natural, takes its name:

Out of his infinite glory, may he give you the power through his Spirit for your hidden self to grow strong, so that Christ may live in your hearts through faith, and then, planted in love and built on love, you will with all the saints have strength to grasp the breadth and the length, the height and the depth; until, knowing the love of Christ, which is beyond all knowledge, you are filled with the utter fullness of God.

Glory be to him whose power, working in us, can do infinitely more than we can ask or imagine; glory be to him from generation to generation in the Church and in Christ Jesus for ever and ever. Amen.

Ephesians 3:14–21

Exercise Nine

How Far Have We Travelled?

Take the usual time and space to prepare yourself for the exercise. You will need the map/castle that we drew earlier.

Having taken some moments for recollection take out the castle you drew at the beginning and see if you feel anything has changed since you drew it. You may like to move some things around, or change or add things. You may even want to draw a completely new map.

When you have finished adjusting the old map or making a new one take a break.

Now consider the differences between the two. What has happened? What has changed during the course of the other exercises? Perhaps nothing has, in which case ask what you would like to have changed given a choice.

When you are ready, take the map and return, in your imagination, to the snowbound inn we entered at the beginning of our journey. Seek out Teresa amongst the crowds in the inn and present her with your new map. You may like to talk to her about some of the things she has discussed through the journey, thank her for some piece of advice, query another or feel like criticizing some points of her approach. Feel free to chat with her – I'm sure she won't mind.

Finally, close with a short prayer; or, if you want to go further, take the map to Christ and present it to him: see what he has to say about it and how you

131

feel about presenting it to him. End with an expression of thanks for anything that has been revealed to you during the course of the journey. You may also want to ask directions for where to travel next: the journey may only just be beginning for you!

✳

Note: All the exercises we have covered are just beginnings. The spiritual processes described by Teresa are profound, long-lasting and may even last a lifetime. See these exercises as springboards to launch you off in new directions – but remember, there's always the force of gravity!

Happy travels!

Appendix

Basic Stillness Exercises

Be still, and know that I am God.
Psalm 46:10

The basis of good prayer is simplicity. If you are finding that a certain method or technique is getting in your way or you are finding it too difficult to grasp, the answer is simple – ditch it! You may find at first that you have to try several different methods and types of prayer before you find those that are most comfortable for you.

There are certain basic exercises which are unbeatable for beginning prayer or just bringing us back to the here and now. They come under a variety of names such as 'stillness exercises', 'centering techniques' or 'silent meditation'. Here are a few which are most frequently used and you may find it useful to return to them even when you are no longer a beginner in prayer. They can all be used in conjunction with any of the exercises in this book.

Basic Body Awareness

This is the simplest and most direct method of centering. I always begin my own prayer with this exercise and never commence a group or workshop without just a few moments of basic body awareness. Make yourself comfortable. Adopt any position that is comfortable to you (e.g. sitting on a chair,

133

sitting cross-legged), but try to have your back straight and erect (it is fine to lie down but not a good idea if you're tired!).

The idea of the exercise is just to be aware of bodily sensations – not to comment on them or think about them. Zen masters talk about the 'monkey mind' – always chattering and distracting us. If these distractions arise, let them pass and remain concentrating on your bodies. Now close your eyes.

Begin with your feet ... feel the pressure of the ground under them, supporting you. If you are sitting feel the energy under your bottom and on the back of the chair holding you up. When you are ready explore the sensations in your legs. Notice the feel of fabric on them or any pressures or tensions. Move slowly from the feet to the upper thighs.

Now notice your hands ... spend some time with the myriad of tiny sensations in your fingers, thumbs, the palm of your hand and so on. Notice feelings of warmth and cold, moisture and dryness. Now move up your arms, noticing the sensations all the way, but don't comment on them. When you reach the top of your arms, spend some time around the armpits, before moving to the shoulders ... move them if there is any tension; shake and allow them to relax.

Be aware of your stomach and chest ... notice the gentle rising and falling motion of your breathing. Follow it a little before moving to the mouth and nose. Notice the breath entering and leaving the body, feel the cool air entering and the warm air leaving.

Now turn your attention to the inside of your mouth. Again, notice all the thousands of sensations in your mouth, around your teeth and around your tongue. Move then to your nose, eyes and forehead.

Finally, end with the very top of your head – the crown. Imagine a thread connecting it with the ceiling and allow the energy to flow up through it. When you are ready, gently open your eyes and relax.

This exercise should have put you in touch with the presence of your body here and now. If you want to focus on one area rather than another, then do so – the above is a rough guide to enable you to find the most comfortable way of being aware of your body. The important thing is not to be thinking too much while it is happening and to be embodied. If you fall asleep, then listen to the message your body is giving you; our bodies have much to tell us if we only but listen to them. If you find yourself getting tense, then just concentrate on that tension and listen to what it is saying to you.

Concentrated Body Awareness

This is a variation and deepening of the above.

Having taken the time to proceed through the bodily sensations as described, choose just one small area of your face and remain with it for five minutes. It may be the tip of the nose, a cheek, the forehead or the lips. As you remain with it just notice the myriad of sensations in that tiny area. You may feel itchy or uncomfortable or want to scratch an area, but resist the temptation as much as you can and just notice the sensations of itchiness – registering them in your consciousness but doing nothing about them. When you are ready open your eyes.

135

This exercise is again very simple, but it can take years to become still enough just to sit with all the sensations in one tiny area. It deepens the concentration.

Breath Awareness

Breath is the very stuff of life. The words for spirit, psyche and soul are all connected with breath. This is also a very simple but powerful exercise.

Take time to relax yourself. You may want to do a short body awareness as above to centre yourself. Make yourself comfortable and close your eyes, then concentrate on your breath.

Notice the gentle sensations as the cold air enters your nostrils. Follow it through as it moves down into your lungs. Now concentrate on the warm air that you breathe out. Again, notice where it is coming from. Be aware of the motion of your chest, gently moving up and down, and notice the steady rhythm of your breathing. It has been going on all through your life, it goes on now and will (hopefully!) continue long after this exercise is finished.

Enjoy the still space this breath awareness gives you and remember you can return to it at any time. Your breathing is always with you.

When you're ready open your eyes.

Stillness of Mind

This exercise is to help create inner peace. It is the mental equivalent of the concentrated body awareness exercise.

Take some time to relax yourself and close your eyes. When you are ready become slowly aware of your thoughts. Spend some time just following them around: *'Oh dear, I hope I turned the heating off.' 'What am I going to cook tonight?' 'What am I doing this for? I've got a thousand and one other things to do.'* Don't comment on them, but simply observe them. When you are ready, choose a simple phrase to repeat over and over again. It may be a religious phrase such as 'Jesus' or 'Jesus, Father, Spirit'. It may be something like 'I am alive' or 'I am thinking'. Be aware of the phrase and allow it to work for you. If possible, choose the first phrase that comes to mind. Don't question it, just let it be. Do this for five to ten minutes.

When you are ready open your eyes.

This form of prayer is called 'using a mantra' and is found in many traditions. It is close to spiritual practices such as the praying of the 'rosary': the repetition of prayers while counting beads.

If you would like further information about this technique see the books by Laurence Freeman and John Main in the Bibliography.

Awareness of Sounds

We used this exercise at the end of chapter three but it is useful to repeat it here. Again it is very simple and very powerful.

Take the time to become still and relaxed. When you have closed your eyes concentrate on all the sounds you can hear around you. Begin with those furthest away: aeroplanes, traffic, birds, street sounds. Move then to the room you are in: the sounds of central heating, people talking, clocks ticking. Finally be aware of the sounds within yourself: your heartbeat, the sound of your breath, the circulation in your ears. When you have spent some time centering in on yourself repeat the process in reverse, moving outwards until you end with the most distant sounds. Now open your eyes.

This exercise will help you become aware of all the complex energies that surround you and the life that is flowing in and around you all the time.

Visual Awareness

Sometimes you may want to use a visual aid to focus your awareness. This can be an object, such as a candle, a picture, a religious representation or ikon. Alternatively you may like to position yourself by a window and concentrate on one object in the distance – a tree or a hill, for example. Whatever object you choose, spend time with it and let it speak to you in its own way. Allow its special message to unfold and to still you.

These are just a few of the many stillness methods available. They are the most basic exercises, but essential. Consider them to be the basic tools in any spiritual 'tool kit'. The greatest spiritual practitioners use them and it seems we never 'grow out of them'. If you would like to explore these exercises in greater depth, Anthony de Mello's *Sadhana* (see Bibliography) is strongly recommended.

Select Bibliography

Teresa and Her Works

All quotations from *The Interior Castle* are from the Hodder and Stoughton Christian Classics edition, edited by Halcyon Backhouse, 1988. I carry this little pocket version around with me everywhere I go and find it very accessible.

For a more detailed version and for the other works of Teresa mentioned (*Life of the Holy Mother Teresa of Jesus*, *The Way of Perfection*, *The Book of Her Foundations*) I would recommend the three volumes of *Complete Works of Saint Teresa of Jesus* translated by E. Allison Peers (Sheed and Ward, 1946).

Alternatively, try *The Collected Works of Teresa of Avila* translated by K. Kavanaugh and O. Rodriguez (ICS, 1985).

There are numerous commentaries on Teresa, some of which I have mentioned as we have gone along.

Good introductions to her life include: *La Madre, The Life and Spirituality of Teresa of Avila* by Elizabeth Ruth Obbard (St Pauls, 1994) and *Teresa of Avila* by Shirley du Boulay (Hodder and Stoughton, 1991).

On her spirituality, I enjoy the works of Tessa Bielecki, especially *Holy Daring: An outrageous gift to modern spirituality from Saint Teresa, the grand, wild woman of Avila* (Element, 1994) and *Teresa of*

Avila, an introduction to her life and writings
(Burns and Oates, 1994). I find that she injects a
great deal of passion into her writings and makes
the saint's spirituality become really alive.

More down-to-earth is *Interior Castle Explored –
St Teresa's Teaching on the Life of Deep Union with
God* by the English Carmelite Ruth Burrows (Sheed
and Ward, 1981). It is thorough and well written.

Finally, on the relation between Teresa and the
psychology of Jung I would strongly recommend
Spiritual Pilgrims: Carl Jung and Teresa of Avila
by John Welch (Paulist, 1982) – an excellent and
ground-breaking work.

On the relation of eros to spirituality I recommend *Mystical Passion: The Art of Christian Loving*
by William McNamara OCD (Element, 1977).

Other Spiritualities

All my quotations from John of the Cross are from
The Collected Works of John of the Cross, translated
by K. Kavanaugh and O. Rodriguez (ICS, 1979).

There are many excellent commentaries on John
but I particularly recommend *The Impact of God,
Soundings from St John of the Cross* by Iain
Matthew (Hodder and Stoughton, 1995).

Also, very relevant to John are *When the Well
runs dry: Prayer beyond the Beginnings* by T. H.
Green SJ (Ave Maria Press, 1979) and two books by
William Johnston SJ: *Being in Love, The Practice of
Christian Prayer* (Fount, 1989) and *Letters to
Contemplatives* (Fount, 1991).

There are numerous versions of the *Spiritual
Exercises of St Ignatius of Loyola*. The standard

translation is by L. J. Puhl SJ (Loyola University Press, 1951). A good modern version is *Modern Spiritual Exercises* by D. L. Fleming SJ (Image, 1978).

An excellent commentary on Ignatian spirituality is *God of Surprises* by Gerard W. Hughes SJ (DLT, 1985) or any of his works such as *Oh God Why?* (Bible Reading Fellowship, 1993) and *Walk to Jerusalem* (DLT, 1990).

The most complete version of the *Rule of St Benedict* is edited by T. Fry OSB (Liturgical Press, 1981).

For more on stillness and the use of the mantra I recommend anything by John Main OSB, especially *The Inner Christ* (DLT, 1987) and by Laurence Freeman OSB such as *The Selfless Self* (DLT, 1993).

Finally, Bede Griffiths OSB was an inspired Benedictine who tried to accomplish a fusion between Eastern and Western spiritualities by moving to India and writing several commentaries on the holy scriptures. *Return to the Centre* (Collins, 1976) and *The Marriage of East and West* (Fount, 1982) are strongly recommended.

The songs of Mirabai are from *For Love of the Dark One* (trans. A. Schelling, Shambala, 1993).

On stillness exercises and meditation I recommend *Sadhana: A Way to God, Christian Exercises in Eastern Form* by Anthony de Mello SJ (Image, 1984). And on the Chakras, *Theories of the Chakras: Bridge to Higher Consciousness* by Hiroshi Motoyama (Quest, 1981).

The annual publication *Vision* gives lists of all places currently available for retreats and other spiritual programmes.

Notes

1 Fire from Heaven

1. Elizabeth Ruth Obbard, *La Madre, The Life and Spirituality of Teresa of Avila*, p. 151
2. *Life of the Holy Mother Teresa of Jesus*, p. 13
3. *Life*, p. 192
4. *Mystical Passion – The Art of Christian Loving*, p. 118
5. *The Way of Perfection*, p. 36
6. *La Madre, The Life and Spirituality of Teresa of Avila*, p. 102
7. In Vol. One of *The Complete Works of Saint Teresa of Jesus*, trans. E. Allison Peers
8. *Teresa of Avila*, Shirley du Boulay, p. 226

2 The First Mansion: Entering the Castle

1. Quoted in *Complete Works*, vol. II, p. 187
2. *Interior Castle*, p. 6
3. *Interior Castle*, p. 14
4. *Interior Castle*, p. 41

3 The Second Mansion: Balance

1. *Interior Castle*, p. 18
2. *Rule of St Benedict*, ch. 39, trans. David Parry
3. *Interior Castle*, p. 55
4. *Interior Castle*, p. 19
5. See Appendix for more information on guides to praying
6. Quoted in John Wijngaard, *Stepping Into The Seven Circles of Prayer*, Housetop, 1993
7. *Interior Castle*, p. 19
8. *Interior Castle*, p. 19
9. *Interior Castle*, p. 21

4 The Third Mansion: Saying and Showing

1. *Interior Castle*, p. 28
2. *Interior Castle*, p. 31
3. *Interior Castle*, p. 32
4. *Interior Castle*, p. 33

5 The Fourth Mansion: On the Edge of Infinity

1. *Interior Castle*, p. 37
2. *Memories, Dreams, Reflections*, p. 223
3. *Memories, Dreams, Reflections*, p. 224
4. *Interior Castle*, p. 44
5. *Life*, p. 65
6. *loc cit.*
7. *Interior Castle*, p. 45
8. *Life*, p. 97
9. *Ibid.*
10. *Interior Castle*, p. 52

6 The Fifth Mansion: The Little Butterfly

1. *Interior Castle*, p. 165
2. *Interior Castle*, p. 57
3. From *Schmetterlinge*, Insel Taschenbuch, 1982, my translation
4. *Interior Castle*, p. 63
5. *Spiritual Pilgrims*, p. 139
6. *Interior Castle*, p. 63
7. *Ibid.*
8. *Spiritual Pilgrims*, p. 140

7 The Sixth Mansion: Visions in the Night

1. John of the Cross, *The Dark Night of the Soul*
2. *Interior Castle*, p. 66
3. *For Love of the Dark One*, trans. A. Schelling, p. 37
4. *Interior Castle*, p. 81
5. This phrase comes from Tessa Bielecki's *Teresa of Avila: an introduction to her life and writings*
6. *Interior Castle*, p. 92

7. *Interior Castle*, p. 93
8. *Interior Castle*, p. 104
9. *Interior Castle*, p. 106
10. *Ibid.*
11. *Interior Castle*, p. 130
12. *Interior Castle*, p. 91
13. *Interior Castle*, p. 73
14. *Interior Castle*, p. 132
15. *Interior Castle*, p. 118
16. *Interior Castle*, p. 121
17. *Interior Castle*, p. 140
18. *The Impact of God*, p. 1
19. See especially *When the Well runs dry*
20. *When the Well runs dry,* p. 121
21. *The Dark Night of the Soul*, Book 2, chapter 6
22. Reprinted in *The Way*, supplement 82: p. 96
23. *The Collected Works of John of the Cross*, p. 313
24. *Ibid.*
25. *Collected Works of John of the Cross*, p. 410
26. *Collected Works of John of the Cross*, p. 313
27. *The Impact of God*, p. 78

8 The Seventh Mansion: The Mystical Marriage

1. *Interior Castle*, p. 145
2. *Interior Castle*, p. 152
3. *Interior Castle*, p. 159
4. *Interior Castle*, p. 49
5. *Interior Castle*, p. 163
6. *Interior Castle*, p. 161
7. *Ibid.*

Epilogue: Back to Life, Back to Reality

1. From *Collected Poems 1909–1962*, Faber and Faber
2. *Interior Castle*, p. 165
3. Quoted in Eric Hobsbawm, *The Age of Extremes: The Short Twentieth Century 1914–1991*, Michael Joseph, 1994, p. 1